TREATING DEPRESSION IN CHILDREN AND ADOLESCENTS

Pergamon Titles of Related Interest

Becker/Heimberg/Bellack SOCIAL SKILLS TRAINING TREATMENT FOR DEPRESSION

Gotlib/Colby TREATMENT OF DEPRESSION: An Interpersonal System Approach

Oster/Caro/Eagen/Lillo ASSESSING ADOLESCENTS

Pope/McHale/Craighead SELF-ESTEEM ENHANCEMENT WITH CHILDREN AND ADOLESCENTS

Van Hasselt/Hersen HANDBOOK OF ADOLESCENT PSYCHOLOGY

Yost/Beutler/Corbishley/Allender GROUP COGNITIVE THERAPY: A Treatment Method for Depressed Older Adults

Related Journal

(Free sample copies available upon request)

CHILD ABUSE AND NEGLECT
CLINICAL PSYCHOLOGY REVIEW
JOURNAL OF CHILD PSYCHOLOGY AND PSYCHIATRY AND ALLIED DISCIPLINES

PSYCHOLOGY PRACTITIONER GUIDEBOOKS

TREATING DEPRESSION IN CHILDREN AND ADOLESCENTS

JOHNNY L. MATSON
Louisiana State University

PERGAMON PRESS
New York • Oxford • Beijing • Frankfurt
São Paulo • Sydney • Tokyo • Toronto

Pergamon Press Offices:

U.S.A.	Pergamon Press, Inc., Maxwell House, Fairview Park, Elmsford, New York 10523, U.S.A.
U.K.	Pergamon Press plc, Headington Hill Hall, Oxford OX3 0BW, England
PEOPLE'S REPUBLIC OF CHINA	Pergamon Press, Qianmen Hotel, Beijing, People's Republic of China
FEDERAL REPUBLIC OF GERMANY	Pergamon Press GmbH, Hammerweg 6, D-6242 Kronberg, Federal Republic of Germany
BRAZIL	Pergamon Editora Ltda, Rua Eça de Queiros, 346, CEP 04011, São Paulo, Brazil
AUSTRALIA	Pergamon Press Australia Pty Ltd., P.O. Box 544, Potts Point, NSW 2011, Australia
JAPAN	Pergamon Press, 8th Floor, Matsuoka Central Building, 1-7-1 Nishishinjuku, Shinjuku-ku, Tokyo 160, Japan
CANADA	Pergamon Press Canada Ltd., Suite 271, 253 College Street, Toronto, Ontario M5T 1R5, Canada

---

Library of Congress Cataloging in Publication Data

Matson, Johnny L.
Treating depression in children and adolescents / Johnny L. Matson.
p. cm. -- (Psychology practitioners guidebooks)
Bibliography: p.
Includes index.
ISBN 0-08-035874-8 : ISBN 0-08-035875-6 (soft)
1. Depression in children. 2. Depression in adolescence. I. Title. II. Series.
[DNLM: 1. Depressive Disorder--in adolescence. 2. Depressive Disorder--in infancy & childhood. 3. Depressive Disorder--therapy. WM 171 M434t]
RJ506.D4M318 1989
618.92′8527--dc19
DNLM/DLC
for Library of Congress 88-29101
CIP

Printed in the United States of America

The paper used in this publication meets the minimum requirements of American National Standard for Information Sciences -- Permanence of Paper for Printed Library Materials, ANSI Z39.48-1984

Dedication

To my wife Deann, and my children, Meggan and Michael.

A special thanks to Vetta M. Johnson who spent many hours typing and revising the manuscript. And to Virginia Fee for reviewing the manuscript for me.

Contents

Preface ix

1. Definition, Diagnosis, and Etiology 1
2. Assessment with Interviews, Direct Observation, and Biological Markers 22
3. Assessment with Checklists 40
4. Treatment: Developing a Treatment Plan and Cognitive Therapy 60
5. Treatment: Social Learning, Operant and Drug Treatments 76

References 93

Author Index 105

Subject Index 109

About the Author 113

Psychology Practitioner Guidebooks Series List 115

Preface

Mental health problems of the population in general and of children in particular have received increasing attention in recent years. The devastating impact that emotional distress has had on the young persons involved, and its spillover effects on the entire family unit, has been documented in recent years. Nowhere has the nature of emotional problems of children been more pronounced than with depression, often referred to as the "common cold" of mental illness due to its frequency. However, only in the last 10 to 15 years has the problem received a good deal of attention from the professional community. Among the serious effects of the disorder are major academic problems in school, severe adjustment and social interaction deficits with friends and family, and suicide or attempted suicide. Obviously, and despite arguments by some in the professional community that childhood depression could not exist, this has become an important topic and one that has been highly studied by mental health professionals in recent years. As a result, an exponential growth in research has occurred. A volume on practical issues of assessment and treatment would therefore seem timely and useful for clinicians, advanced graduate students, and researchers.

The present volume is an effort to provide an up-to-date review of the best information that is available on psychological principles and procedures that may prove useful in the treatment of childhood depression. An effort has been made to stress the research done on various assessment and treatment methods. However, there are likely to be a variety of other assessment and treatment methods for depression in widespread use. It is important to stress procedures that have been systematically tested to separate those methods which are beneficial from those that are not. This approach eliminates some of the guesswork in therapy, although it is also true that a fly-by-the-seat-of-your-pants, trial-and-error approach will always be the case to some extent, given the idiosyncratic nature of emotional problems. However, the use of research-based methods should result in fewer unsuccessful attempts since the therapist knows that the assessment and treatment procedures have proven effective in at least some instances with clients similar to the persons being treated. It can be argued that an educated guess provides a reasonable starting point.

This book should not be seen as the only means of working with depressed children. However, it should serve as information likely to prove useful as a case of systematically compiled data for assessment and treatment planning. And, sufficient research seems to have emerged to date so that a number of data-based assessment and treatment procedures are now in place. Most research in the next few years is likely to focus on refining these procedures. Hopefully this book will serve a useful purpose for professionals working with children and their families suffering from emotional stress.

Johnny L. Matson, Ph.D.
Professor of Psychology
Louisiana State University
Baton Rouge, Louisiana 70803

Chapter 1

Definition, Diagnosis, and Etiology

Depression, in general terminology, can refer to severe mood swings or to mild variations in affect. In the clinical context, which will be the reference point for this book, depression refers not only to a state of depression but to a syndrome with psychomotor and somatic/vegetative states lasting weeks or months. Additionally, clinically significant depression generally affects the person's ability to live a normal life. Persons may lose interest in school, friends, television programs, and other activities previously enjoyed. Unlike other disorders, such as schizophrenia, that adversely affect thought, the principal symptoms of depression are mood and affect. Typical of these symptoms are sadness, low self-esteem, and loss of interest in activities. The disorder occurs so frequently that it is referred to as the "common cold of emotional problems." Thus, a book pertaining to this problem in youth should be of interest to all mental health workers who deal with children and adolescents.

For adults,the concept of depression as a syndrome and as a disorder is well accepted (Cantwell, 1983). However, one difficulty is that the symptoms occur on a continuum, with all persons evincing some depressive characteristics at some point in time. The problem is to identify where normality ends and clinical depression begins so that those with a serious problem can be identified and treated. Andreasen (1982) has discussed this issue, stressing length of symptom display and cooccurrence of several symptoms as key issues at any age.

As just mentioned, the way in which problems affect normal routines for the client should be an issue. Symptom identification is of course central to the field of childhood depression. A concern in childhood psychopathology involved the effort to transfer symptoms observed in adults to children and youth as a means of describing the phenomenon in younger age groups. This approach was attempted with childhood depression but resistance existed on two levels. First, some argued that children's symptoms were unique and should not be evaluated in the same way as those of adults. Second, some professionals argued against the existence of the disorder (Rehm, Leventon, and Ivens, 1987). It was their contention that childhood depression could not exist because it was a superego phenomenon. These psychoanalytic writers stressed the idea that children did not have proper superego development, thus obviating the presence of the condition in children (Rochlin, 1959; Beres, 1966). However, with the development of empirically based instruments to study the disorder, childhood depression became a generally accepted clinical entity by 1980. And the symptoms used to describe the condition are now similar to those of adults. Following is a review of the behaviors comprising childhood depression as they emerged from this controversy among professionals.

METHODS OF EVALUATION

Diagnostic Systems

There is no best way of diagnosing or classifying depression in children. Several systems of classification have been developed with considerable overlap among them. The most popular of these systems is the *Diagnostic and Statistical Manual* (DSM-III-R) (American Psychiatric Association, 1987). Because of the widespread acceptance of this scheme for the diagnosis of other disorders by mental health professionals, it is most certainly a method that the readers should be familiar with.

From an historical standpoint, the Washington University group from the Department of Psychiatry in St. Louis, Missouri, was the first to make extensive clinical efforts to develop assessment and diagnosis procedures in this area. Their early work in categorization led to the DSM-III criteria, which were named after the senior investigator of the group and called the Feighner criteria. This system of symptoms was the starting point of an operationally defined diagnostic taxonomy including childhood depression. A later extrapolation of these criteria was called the Research Diagnostic Criteria (RDC) (Spitzer, Endicott, and Robins, 1978). The Feighner (system 1) and RDC (system 2) criteria were used in research. The DSM-III and DSM-III-R (system 3) criteria were developed by a committee, primarily for use by clinicians. Additionally, both systems were based on the Kraeplinian model of psychopathology developed almost a century before. However, in practice, all the criteria have been used in research and for clinical work, with DSM, as noted earlier, being by far the most popular. For the interested reader, Table 1-1 compares and contrasts the criteria for these three systems. It will be noted that the subject matter across systems is very similar.

At this time, it appears that DSM-III-R is used more often, and that the other systems, because of their similarity, are being phased out.

To this point, we have reviewed the diagnostic systems used primarily in the United States. It should also be noted that the European community in particular has used a system entitled the International Classification of Disease revision 9 (ICD-9). Rutter and Gould (1985) stated that there have been neither reliability nor validity studies for the ICD-9, and that most diagnostic categories have never been the subject of any substantial study. This assumption is supported by others who point out that Feighner, RDC, DSM-III, and DSM-III-R have similar problems. The entire field of diagnosis, then, requires additional study by professionals, with information obtained through research used to refine diagnostic methods.

The clinical systems described above are one of two major diagnostic methods. Some forms of psychopathology have also been substantiated empirically via factor analysis. Empirically derived systems of classification of general childhood psychopathology have emerged and are perhaps best exemplified by Quay and Peterson's Behavior Problem Checklist whose diagnostic categories are presented in Table 1-2 (Quay, 1979; Quay & Peterson, 1975). A brief review of the factors and diagnoses shows that this factored system is not very similar to major diagnostic categories in previously mentioned systems. And the systems subscribed to by clinicans, such as DSM-III, are vastly more popular in everyday use. The question then becomes, given the reality of the situation, how to empirically validate the popular clinical systems by modifying them, since they have and will continue to have the broadest use. This task might be accomplished by modifying and substantiating as much of each diagnostic category as possible without developing new and radically different diagnostic categories such as the Behavior Problem Checklist. Reviews of emerging empirical literature indicate that this latter approach seems to be the most commonly accepted strategy.

Some research has been conducted that demonstrates a unified set of depressive symptoms. Strauss, Forehand, Frame, and Smith (1984), for example, found 15 children (9 females and 6 males) with significant depressive symptoms from a sample of 641. They stated that these children evinced many of the characteristics commonly believed to be associated with childhood and adult depression using DSM-III criteria, including low self-esteem, anxiety, problems with attention and concentration, and difficulties with social relationships. Anxiety was particularly

Table 1–1. Criteria for childhood depression using the most common diagnostic systems

Feighner	Spitzer-RDC
A. Dysphoric Mood-Depressed, sad, discouraged, despondent, irritable, etc. B. Other features. At least five of the following: 1. Poor appetite and weight loss 2. Sleep difficulty (insomnia or hypersomnia) 3. Loss of energy 4. Agitation or retardation 5. Loss of interest in usual activities (including sexual drive) 6. Feelings of self-reproach or guilt 7. Diminished ability to think or concentrate 8. Recurrent thoughts of death or suicide	A. One or more distinct periods of dysphoric mood, pervasive loss of interest, or pleasure. B. At least five of the following: 1. Appetite increase/decrease 2. Sleep disturbance: insomnia, hypersomnia 3. Loss of energy, fatigability 4. Psychomotor agitation or retardation 5. Loss of interest/pleasure in social contact or sex 6. Self-reproach or guilt 7. Diminished ability to think, concentrate 8. Recurrent thoughts of death, suicide
DSM-III	
A. Dysphoric mood or anhedonia B. Other symptoms: at least four of the following: 1. Appetite/weight gain/loss 2. Sleep difficulty 3. Loss of energy 4. Loss of interest or pleasure in usual activity 5. Self-reproach, inappropriate guilt 6. Diminished concentration 7. Suicidal tendencies C. Duration: At least two weeks D. Exclusions: 1. Schizophrenic symptoms 2. Organic mental disorder 3. Residual-type schizophrenia 4. Simple bereavement	
C. Duration: at least 1 month with no other preexisting psychiatric condition or medical illness that could account for depressive symptomatology D. There are patients who fulfill the above criteria, but also have a massive or peculiar alteration of perception and thinking as a major manifestation of their illness. These patients are currently classified as having a schizoaffective psychosis	C. Duration: At least one week D. Sought help, medicated functional impairment E. Exclusion criteria suggesting schizophrenia: 1. Delusions discordant for depression 2. Nonaffective hallucinations for several days or intermittently for a week 3. Auditory hallucinations 4. More than one month of delusions or hallucinations without Spitzer RDC 5. Preoccupation with delusion or hallucinations discordant for depression 6. Formal thought disorders

Table 1–2. Condensed versions of the Weinberg and Feighner symptoms for childhood depression

Major Symptoms and Behavioral Components

I. Dysphoric Mood (Melancholy)
  a. Statements or appearance of sadness, loneliness, unhappiness, hopelessness, and/or pessimism
  b. Mood swings, moodiness
  c. Irritable, easily annoyed
  d. Hypersensitive, cries easily
  e. Negative, difficult to please

II. Self-deprecatory Ideation
  a. Feeling of being worthless useless, dumb, stupid, ugly, guilty (negative self-concept)
  b. Beliefs of persecution
  c. Death wishes
  d. Desire to run away or leave home
  e. Suicidal thoughts
  f. Suicidal attempts

III. Aggressive Behavior (Agitation)
  a. Difficult to get along with
  b. Quarrelsome
  c. Disrespectful of authority
  d. Belligerent, hostile, agitated
  e. Excessive fighting or sudden anger

IV. Sleep Disturbance
  a. Initial insomnia
  b. Restless sleep
  c. Terminal insomnia
  d. Difficulty waking in morning

V. Change in School Performance
  a. Frequent complaints from teachers re: daydreaming, poor concentration, poor memory
  b. Loss of usual work effort in school subject
  c. Loss of usual interest in nonacademic school activities

VI. Diminished Socialization
  a. Decreased group participation
  b. Less friendly, less outgoing
  c. Socially withdrawing
  d. Loss of usual social interests

VII. Change in Attitude Toward School
  a. Does not enjoy school activities
  b. Does not want or refuses to attend school

VIII. Somatic Complaints
  a. Nonmigraine headaches
  b. Abdominal pain
  c. Muscle aches or pains
  d. Other somatic concerns or complaints

XI. Loss of Usual Energy
  a. Loss of usual personal interests or pursuits other than school: e.g., hobbies
  b. Decreased energy: mental and/or physical fatigue

X. Usual Change in Appetite and/or Weight
  a. Anorexia or polyphagia
  b. Unusual weight change in past four months

evident, and teachers noted that these children could be readily separated on this dimension from other children in their classes. Moreover, Seagull and Weinshank (1984) found that in addition to being anxious, the 82 seventh graders they identified as having depressed affect also avoided tasks and were less socially competent than other children. Their parents had less schooling than the norm and were more likely to use corporal punishment. These items and those presented in the major diagnostic systems reviewed provide the basis for core symptoms of this condition.

Related Systems

DSM is the most popular method that has been employed in this country. There are, however, other approaches that have been employed, and these are of note in the development of diagnostic methods.

As mentioned earlier, two systems of symptom identification related to DSM-III are the Weinberg (Weinberg, Rutman, Sullivan, Penick, & Dietz, 1973) and Feighner criteria (Feighner, Robins, Guze, Woodruff, Winokur, & Munoz, 1972). These methods have been condensed by Brumback, Dietz-Schmidt, and Weinberg (1977). They list the major depressive symptoms observed in children as dysphoric mood, self-deprecation, aggression, sleep disturbance, change in school performance, diminished socialization, changes in attitude toward school, somatic complaints, loss of energy, and changes in appetite and/or weight. Based on these systems developed through clinical work and some research, the DSM-III criteria emerged. The similarity of all three of these categorization systems can be noted. Table 1-3 gives a more detailed description of symptoms that fall under the general category of depression in children when a composite of these approaches is used. These symptons had been employed to define the disorder before DSM-III, and were often noted in research studies on childhood depression. When DSM-III appeared, the influence of criteria external to the DSM system began to decrease in popularity. At this writing, they are no longer referred to frequently.

Research on Related Factors

More research needs to be conducted for further refinement of the still-evolving DSM diagnostic system, given that what has been done to date has only scratched the surface of knowledge about childhood depression, and that this system is used almost without exception in clinical settings. A brief review of some topics related to the centrally identified symptoms follows. This research does not necessarily present a priority

Table 1-3. Anthony and Scott criteria for bipolar depression in children

1. Evidence of an abnormal psychiatric state at some time of the illness approximating the 1921 Kraepelinian criteria
2. Evidence of a positive family history
3. Early tendency to a manic depressive reaction with a cyclothymic tendency for gradually increasing amplitude and length of oscillations and delirious manic or depressive outbursts occurring during pyrexial illness
4. Recurrent or periodic illness of at least two episodes
5. Major swings in dimensions of pathology
6. Low tolerance to environmental events
7. Severe illness requiring hospitalization
8. Abnormal extroverted personality
9. Lack of schizophrenia or organicity
10. Current rather than retrospetive assessment

list of the most relevant issues but it will undoubtedly indicate some important areas where additional research would be of use in further clarifying depression in children and youth.

The equivalent of work for children is academic functioning. School performance is an important factor that should be looked at in identifying childhood depression. A sudden (over several weeks) drop in academic achievement from the child's normal performance level is not conclusive evidence but is, most certainly, a strong indicator of childhood depression when some of the other symptoms noted above are also evident. This problem might typically be exhibited as loss of interest in important daily activities. Tesiny, Lefkowitz, and Gordon (1980) have been among the researchers to empirically confirm this point. Thus, as a related clinical issue it should certainly be considered.

Another related problem is aggression. Some have argued that this condition is a form of masked depression. Although such an assumption is not endorsed here, it would be possible to suggest that overlap with depression is possible and perhaps likely for some children. Often, irritability accompanies childhood depression. This, along with frustration, might result in acting out at home and in the school.

Interestingly, nonverbal behavior correlates only moderately with childhood depression while it is much more highly related to the disorder among adults. This finding is at odds with a general assumption that childhood behavior is more clearly displayed nonverbally and might be yet another way (e.g., school performance, aggression) in which childhood problems differ from those of adults. Responses of 16 psychiatric inpatient children, ages 5 to 13, were assessed in the one study conducted to date on this issue (Kazdin, Sherick, Esveldt-Dawson, & Rancurello, 1985). Nonverbal behaviors found to be associated with depression included facial expression, body movements, head shaking, hand and arm gestures used in speech, and tearfulness. These behaviors were evident in boys and girls. However, girls also had less eye contact, smiled less, and more often evinced flat intonation in speech.

While more research is required on the range of depressive characteristics in children, the behaviors identified here point out a need for further empirical verification and a necessity to identify a variety of interrelated responses that can be used to confirm or refute a diagnosis of depression in young persons.

CONTROVERSIES IN DIAGNOSIS

Existence of Childhood Depression

All areas of science have topics of controversy, and childhood depression is no exception. For example, Lefkowitz and Burton (1978) proposed three general assumptions about the depressed child: (1) if behaviors thought to constitute depression are prevalent in normal children, they cannot be considered pathological and, therefore, the syndrome does not exist; (2) if behaviors thought to constitute the syndrome disappear over time, they cannot be considered pathological; and, (3) problems that remit spontaneously do not require treatment. Those who wish to employ an extremely conservative view of depression might consider such an approach. However, a more liberal interpretation in diagnosing depression has also been presented which is at the other extreme of the continuum with many more symptoms being characterized as depression. A closer look at some of the assumptions discussed follow.

Masked Depression

The opposite extreme of the contention that childhood depression does not exist came from those who placed most childhood psychopathology into the category of masked depression. This definition of depression exemplifies a much wider description of the disorder. And, as a diagnostic entity, masked depression was a controversial topic that received a good deal of professional attention in the first half of the 1980s. Today it is not a popularly accepted concept. It had been proposed that children, in their attempts to ward off depressive feelings, would mask the condition by exhibiting characteristics of aggression (Cytryn & McKnew, 1974; Lesse, 1974). Proponents argued that a depressed mood is not sustained because the child cannot tolerate prolonged feelings of sadness. In diagnosing masked depression, it was proposed that the presenting problem should be associated with symptoms of depression while, concurrently, evidence of depression in the child's dreams, fantasies, and verbal content should be identified (Rehm, Leventon, & Ivens, 1988). Thus, outwardly it would be hard to differentiate masked depression from other problems such as conduct disorder.

Masked depression has been severely criticized and in general has lost favor among most researchers and clinicians in the field (Bemporad, 1978; Carlson & Cantwell, 1980; Cytryn, McKnew, & Bunny, 1980). The difficulty with this approach is that, by accepting the hypothesis, almost all deviant behavior of childhood becomes depression. And common disorders such as hyperactivity and conduct disorder no longer are distinct childhood problems. However, an alternative explanation exists. It is apparent that two or more childhood disorders may coexist, with one of these being depression (Carlson, 1983a). Matson and Nieminen (1987) have been among the authors to empirically demonstrate what has become an accepted alternate diagnostic formation for some. In tests of 95 students, ages 11 to 18, who were receiving services in a private school for conduct disorders, over one third also met criteria for depression on the Child Depression Inventory and the Reynolds Adolescent Depression Scale. Similarly, Kashani et al. (1987), in another study on the same topic, sampled 150 adolescents 14 to 16 years of age. From this sample, 28 adolescents were diagnosed as psychiatrically impaired and evinced considerable overlapping of the symptoms of depression, conduct disorder, anxiety, and oppositional disorder. Figure 1-1 from this study pictorially represents the coexistence of various forms of child psychopathology.

Jacobsen, Lahey, and Strauss (1983) also observed an overlapping of various problems and depression. Among these problems were unpopularity with peers and somatic complaints. Based on these results it would seem then that covariation of various symptoms and some overlap in emotional disorders (with one of these being depression) may exist.

Norvell and Towle (1986) also recognized this phenomenon of coexisting psychopathology. They studied 56 boys, 9 to 12 years of age, via the Behavior Problem Checklist and the Child Depression Inventory (CDI). There was considerable relation between the two scales with respect to the severity of symptoms for a given client. An interesting point these authors made is that several CDI items reflect conduct problems. On items of the CDI such as depressed mood, self-deprecation, rumination, or social withdrawal, no such overlap was evident. The authors therefore concluded that there are similarities in some essential features of both conditions.

These data therefore seem to support the hypothesis that depression is a distinct disorder, although not entirely separate from other conditions. The concept of overlapping conditions should be considered.

Suicide

Arguably the most severe aspect of depression in children and youth is the potential for suicide. The potential for this condition to develop exists; the result can be serious injury, long-term physical or mental-

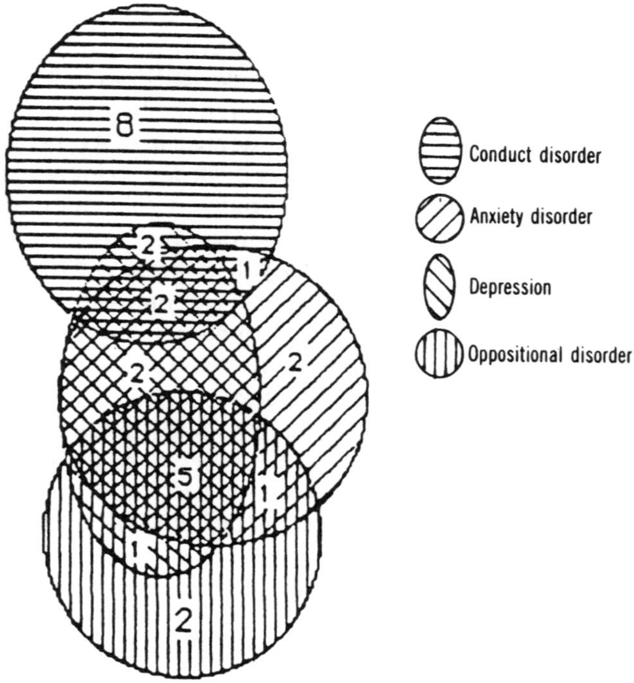

FIGURE 1–1. Pictorial representation of overlap in diagnostic categories of childhood psychopathology. (*American Journal of Psychiatry, 144*: 584-589. Copyright 0000, The American Psychiatric Association. Reprinted by permission.)

disabilities, or even death. Suicidal ideation and intent are usually associated with unipolar depression in adolescents. Also, and unfortunately, the rate of childhood and adolescent suicide has increased markedly in recent years (Hawton & Osborn, 1984). While successful suicide is more likely to be seen in adolescents and only infrequently occurs in children (Arieti & Bemporad, 1978; Joffe and Offord, 1983), suicidal gestures and threats are common across age groups (Shaffer, 1974; Pfeffer, Conte, Plutchik, & Jerret, 1980). Shaffer (1974) for example, stated that such problems account for 7% to 10% of referrals to child guidance clinics and Pfeffer et al. (1980) found that 33% of children referred to an outpatient clinic had attempted suicide. Although this seems to be an extremely high rate, Pfeffer, Solomon, Plutchik, Mizruchi, and Weiner (1982) reported that 78.5% of all 6 to 12 year olds admitted to a small inpatient unit manifested suicidal ideation or gestures. It should be emphasized that these criteria are somewhat subjective and do not indicate that an attempt actually occurred. Nonetheless, even if these estimates are grossly high, most would agree that the problem is sufficiently common to be of great concern.

Of particular interest in the diagnosis of suicidal behavior in children and adolescents is its relationship to the same problem among adults. Unlike general depressive symptoms, suicidal behavior appears to differ markedly from adults to youngsters (Arieti & Bemporad, 1978). Although suicide attempts are greater for boys than for girls, suicidal talk increases with age, particularly among girls (Shectman, 1970). In a recent study, patterns of suicidal symptoms by age and sex were studied more extensively. Bettes and Walker (1986) found that many of the younger boys they evaluated showed none of the conventional warning signs seen in adults. Rather, conduct disorder symptoms were evident. This finding is not particularly comforting to the clinician because it becomes very difficult in these instances to distinguish between the acting-out child and the potentially suicidal child. Compared to boys, girls were more likely to display typical symptoms of presuicide attempts seen in adults. These signs include verbalizations of unhappiness and verbal suicide threats, suicidal gestures, and overt manifestations of depression.

At present we can conclude that it is more difficult to make a prediction of suicide in children and adolescents, based on an observation of depressive symptoms, than it is to make the same prediction in adults. In some instances, however, there are indicators and they should be monitored *very carefully*. It is better to err by acting too quickly than failing to act. Parents and others who may be important to the child should be enlisted to provide emotional support. These persons will need counseling by the professional regarding the best way to interact with the child. Psychological interventions should bring up and review the importance of not becoming overly emotional, of not paying too much attention to the suicidal ideation by constantly bringing it up to the child, and the danger of failing to make efforts to get the child involved in prosocial activities. Primary emphasis should be on providing emotional support and reinforcing prosocial activities. Parents should also be instructed to remove from the home or secure possible means, such as weapons and medications. Also emphasized should be frequent visits to the clinician during critical times of emotional stress, with brief hospitalization as a last resort. The school should be involved including teachers, counselors, and peers.

TYPES OF DEPRESSION

Unipolar versus bipolar depression is another special issue worthy of discussion. Unipolar depression (also referred to as a major depressive episode) is defined by the absence of prior manic or hypomanic episodes. Bipolar depression (manic depressive psychosis) conversely is defined by the presence of major mood swings (Willner, 1985). The general acceptance of the unipolar-bipolar diagnostic groups has been reinforced by the differences found between these two groups. For instance, family history is stronger in the bipolar disorder (Perris, 1966). More recent studies have continued to show that unipolar depressives do not have a family history of bipolar depression. However, bipolar depression may frequently have unipolar depression among family members (Taylor & Abrams, 1986; Tsuang, 1978). Research with children and adolescents evincing bipolar depression is lacking. Carlson (1983b) states that there is little doubt that bipolar depression occurs with some frequency, and cases have been reported in early adolescence. Prepubertal onset, however, is rare.

Anthony and Scott (1960), in reviewing the literature on bipolar depression, used the criteria listed in Table 1-3. They identified three cases of children under 11 years of age with these symptoms, using the approach just described. It seems plausible to assume a much higher rate of unipolar than bipolar depression in children, which probably accounts for the almost complete attention of researchers on the former condition, a bias also evident in this book.

Several loosely developed diagnoses of bipolar depression in children have been reported in addition to those in Table 3, typically within a case description. A common and, in fact, instrumental aspect of the diagnosis was the presence of a family history of some form of depression, cyclothymia, alcoholism, or suicide (Carlson, 1983b). Elated mood was rarely reported, and for younger children (generally prepubertal), irritability, aggression, grandiosity, hallucinations, and emotional liability were pronounced. Looking depressed or complaining of depression was rarely noted. Carlson (1983b) stresses that grandiosity and hallucinations in the child in imaginative play might sometimes be inaccurately seen as aberrant behavior. Thus, developmental milestones should be an important consideration. This comment leads to the next important special issue regarding childhood depression, developmental course.

DEVELOPMENTAL COURSE

Developmental Issues

Unlike adults, only a year's advance in age can radically alter the significance of various behaviors evinced by a child. Across the age span some dramatic differences are evident. As one example, a two year old who frequently becomes tearful may be displaying normal behavior while in a 14 year old the same behavior may be a symptom of depression. Until recently, this problem had been neither recognized nor fully explored with regard to general childhood psychopathology (Achenbach, 1978b) or childhood depression (Rutter, Izard, & Read, 1986). Obviously, better delineated norms for various symptoms of depression are needed.

Rutter (1986) has discussed the variation in rates of depressive symptoms across age. For 10 year olds there were three cases of depression in a sample of 2,000 children, while at ages 14 to 15 there were 9 cases of pure depression and 26 cases of mixed affective disorder. In another study, Pearce (1978) examined 547 inpatient children. Approximately 1 in 9 prepubertal children showed depressive symptoms and 1 in 4 postpubertal children manifested depression.

Based on these developmental phenomenon, two issues should be contemplated by the clinician. First, the form of the disorder may vary across age. And second, the number of depressed persons will likely be much higher among adolescents than among young children. Furthermore, the sex ratio, which is likely to be similar in prepubertal children, shifts such that higher rates of depression are seen in girls at puberty. This issue is very complex, and many theoretical formulations related to developmental phenomena and formulations exist. The interested reader is referred to Rutter et al. (1986) for an extensive review of this topic. Other important issues exist as well. One of these, parental behavior, is briefly outlined next.

Parental Issues.

Parental behavior appears to be a significant issue in childhood depression. Brody and Forehand (1986), in one recent study, found that parents who evinced depression were more likely to have children with conduct disorders or other deviant behavior when compared to parents without emotional problems. Other problems of children whose parents are depressed include being shy and withdrawn, having low comprehension, attention, creativity, patience, academic performance, and, of course, depression (Billings & Moos, 1983; Panaccione & Whaler, 1986). As Morrison (1983) points out, the child is often caught up in the mother's life, and this may have negative manifestations when the parent is suffering from an emotional problem. One side effect is the lack of attention and reinforcement that results from general apathy and failure to act. When the mother is depressed (which is more likely than is the case with the father) the child may react by becoming increasingly more precocious, angry, and aggressive. Also, the child may become depressed himself/herself. Whatever the cause, the depressed parent does seem to put the child at increased risk for depression and a variety of other childhood behavior problems. Thus, a thorough family history and active intervention to treat the parent may in some cases be indicated for the child with depression. Family support may prove to be, if not the most important aspect of the treatment, certainly one of the most important aspects.

SUMMARY

This section of Chapter 1 has reviewed the symptoms of depression and the factors that should be considered in diagnosis. It is heartening that considerable evaluation concerning the nature of this disorder has occurred in but a brief time period. A rather focused definition seems to have emerged recently, and while some modifications will likely occur, this definition will probably be the most popular one for some time. An additional issue is the complexity of the topic. Developmental, gender-related, and other factors have been identified along with environmental factors such as parental behavior. These all suggest the need for a systematic and well-thought-out approach. Another important issue is the frequency with which this condition appears and is addressed next.

PREVALENCE OF CHILDHOOD DEPRESSION

The prevalence or rate of occurrence of a disorder at a given point in time is a topic that has been studied only recently. From published studies, the percentage of children identified as depressed varies widely. Bipolar depression, for example, has not been studied in childhood to any substantial degree. Additionally, there have been no large-scale studies for prevalence figures (Carlson, 1983a). From the few small-scale epidemiological investigations conducted, it would appear that the problem is not major. Kasanin and Kaufman (1929), for example, found that only 1% to 2% of 14 to 18 year olds admitted for psychiatric disturbance suffered from this disorder. Olsen (1961) observed a 6.2% rate in psychiatric patients 13 to 19 years of age, while Landolt (1957) followed 60 cases that had been identified between 13 and 22 years of age. And, some cases studied have appeared in the literature (Carlson & Strober, 1978; Hassanyeh & Davison, 1980). These data present evidence that bipolar depression is evident in children, particularly in postpuberty. Symptoms are similar to those observed in adults and in several instances the afflicted persons had borderline-to-mild mental retardation. Family histories as one might expect were often positive for affective disorders. It is fair to say, however, that bipolar depression has been an issue receiving less attention than unipolar depression. This situation is perhaps due to the recognition that the latter disorder occurs with much greater regularity (Costello, 1980).

To embellish the serious nature and extent of unipolar depression in children is important. In at least one report, 59% of inpatient children were depressed (Kashani et al., 1981). In a comprehensive review by the National Institute of Mental Health, it was concluded that prevalence rates of moderate to severe depression in children ranged from almost no occurrence to 33% (Teuting, Koslow, & Hirschfeld, 1982). In a more recent study, data on 3,020 elementary school children were obtained with 5.2% meeting criteria for depression (Lefkowitz & Tesiny, 1985). The differences in diagnostic criteria, ages of the children, socioeconomic status of families, and many other factors are likely to contribute to the wide disparity in studies reported to date.

Data has also been compiled recently on preschool children. Kashani and Carlson (1987) evaluated 1,000 preschoolers 3 to 6 years of age using DSM-III diagnoses. Depression was evident in only 9 children from this sample. It would appear that with very young children, depression as currently conceptualized is rare.

At this point in time, the frequency of unipolar depression in children is open to debate. However, most researchers and clinicians agree on one point: This problem is a serious one that deserves attention from child clinicians. Thus, professionals who work in the child and adolescent area should be well versed in depression, what causes it, and how best to assess and treat the disorder in children.

THEORIES OF DEPRESSION

Formulations of what causes depression are important in helping professionals understand how depression develops and how it might be treated, prevented, and diagnosed. There have been a number of theoretical formulations, and some research to this regard. Existing theories can be broadly classified into two areas, biological and psychological. A brief review of important concepts follows.

Biological Bases of Depression

Biochemistry. There have been a number of biological factors related to adult depression. Among these are developmental history, plasma cortisol concentrations and growth hormone response in insulin-induced hypoglycemia, urinary MHPG excretions, family psychiatric history, and response to antidepressant medications. The trend in psychiatry has been away from psychological and toward biological explanations and treatments (Coryell, 1987). This approach may largely be due to an emphasis on pharmacological interventions by some in the medical profession. However, and unfortunately, it is the case that most of our knowledge on childhood depression is based on extrapolations from the adult literature. Thus, confidence about the efficacy of this approach with children is limited at best.

Perhaps the most compelling argument for a biological perspective is developmental course, a topic noted earlier in the chapter. While data are still open to various interpretations, it is known that rate and severity of depression does increase with age into adolescence. Undoubtedly, environment and learning play a substantial role, but the biology of maturation seems to be strongly intertwined with the nature of depression. Along these same lines, we know that a family history of depression is closely linked with the manifestation of this disorder in children and adolescence.

Environmental issues regarding family style may also be important factors and are addressed later in this chapter. However, it is unlikely that these environmental issues account for all the variance. It is also true that the biological explanation tends to be most salient when depression is extreme.

Most research in this area has been exploratory and speculative. This situation is to be expected, given that depression has only recently been identified as problematic in children. Puig-Antich (1983) reports data for bipolar depressive adolescents with cortisol hypersecretion. These data, while inconsistent, suggest the possibility of biochemical irregularities as reported with adults. Following research with adults, hyposecretion of growth hormone in response to insulin-induced hypoglycemia have been noted. Based on these findings, Puig-Antich (1983) concluded that neuroendocrine results validate the existence of prepubertal major depression and its similarity to adult major depression.

Physiology. On a psychophysiological level, sleep disturbance has been studied, overall pattern and REM being paramount among changes noted in depressed persons (Kupfer & Foster, 1972). However, with children, the results have been mixed and show a pattern less clearly than with adults.

To date, the biological bases of depression with neuroendocrine and physiological factors and family history are interesting and show promise for further exploration. However, it is also true that the data are descriptive and have no established underlying theoretical formulation to tie these factors together. Formulations of this nature await further study.

Family history would seem to support biochemical and physiological theories of depression. A good deal has been written on the topic, but the general conclusion that can be reached at this point is that the child of a depressed adult runs considerable risk of also evincing the disorder (Bemesderfer & Cohler, 1983; Billings & Moos, 1983; Connors, Himmelhock, Goyette, Ulrich, & Neil, 1979; Weissman et al., 1984). These studies and reviews have generally found a high rate of depression and other impairments in children of depressed parents. Of course, lifestyle is another consideration, and depressed parents' behavior may dramatically affect that of their children. Adoption studies have also shown a higher loading of depression with children and their biological parents (Cantwell, 1983). It should be emphasized, however, that an interaction effect obviously exists. Studies with children of depressed parents in treatment are needed to determine if parental improvement results in enhanced behavior of the child as well. This contention is probably noteworthy and deserves careful attention. It may serve as a prevention model for childhood depression.

Development. One area undoubtedly including a biological factor is human development. Given the long history of developmental psychology and medicine, a hypothesis for the utility of this model to depressive disorders in children and adolescents is much easier to establish. The primary issue here is the continuity of symptoms across ages. As pointed out earlier, suicide threats and attempts increase with age from childhood to adolescence. The most commonly accepted perspective is that development proceeds in an orderly fashion, from a state of relative global responsiveness and lack of differentiation to increased complexity and organization. Psychopathology occurs when lack of integration and orderly development is present. Bemporad and Wilson (1978) stated that the emotions a child can experience are determined by his or her level of cognitive development. It is their opinion that the primary effect of depression will parallel the child's cognitive development. To date, little research on childhood depression has been performed to delineate specific differences across age groups. The specification of these factors awaits study.

ENVIRONMENTAL MODELS

Considerable speculation has occurred regarding environmental/psychological explanations of depressive phenomenon. Nature-nurture factors undoubtedly exist in all cases of childhood and adolescent depression. The environmental issues are likely to be of greater concern with unipolar depression, which constitutes most cases of depression for children and adolescents. Three major theories falling under this general domain will be reviewed: self-regulation, learned helplessness, and Lewinsohn's social learning approach.

Self-regulation

This model, which fits into the self-control camp of behavior therapy, has received a good deal of attention (Kanfer, 1970, 1971; Rehm, 1977). The theory has several general assumptions, the most important of which is that environmental stimulation and momentary environmental events are regulated by biological variables that produce behavior.

Their relevant contribution varies at any given time to produce behavior in a dynamic and fluid fashion. Behavior and decisions are based on short-term and long-term concerns and situations based on internal or external control. How observed information is symbolized and interpreted is of paramount importance. It is felt that the depressed person is more likely to dwell on negative versus positive aspects of his/her environment. There is also the issue of whether events are attributed to external uncontrolled events or are internal and, therefore, controllable by having the child make choices about his/her behavior. The internal/external control of events is sometimes referred to as attribution. The perceived situation is further broken down into short-term and long-term goals. Short-term gratification versus long-term success would be another way of stating this concept.

An effective treatment rests largely on determining etiology. For example, what are the environmental and related biological mechanisms controlling behavior. The focus would then be to teach the client how to control his environment via change of personal choices and his perception of the environment. These factors would then be systematically regulated to enhance social performance. The approach describes one of the closest relations between treatment and etiology. More on this model will be presented later in this book in a discussion concerning treatment.

Learned Helplessness

Learned helplessness, as a theory, has in the past been a popular explanation of depressive behavior. A number of problems were identified in the initial formulation leading to modifications and to the current model (Seligman, 1981). It is argued in the most recent version that depression is defined by four sets of deficits; motivational, cognitive, affective-somatic and self-esteem. There are several premises to the theory, including: (1) The individual expects that highly aversive outcomes are probable or that highly desired outcomes are improbable; (2) The individual expects that no response in his or her repertoire will change the likelihood of these events; (3) Failure is attributed to internal events but success is represented via external causes; (4) The strength of the motivational and cognitive deficits of depression depends jointly on the strength of expectation of an aversive outcome and on the strength of the uncontrollable expectancy. Also, it may be recalled by the reader familiar with this theoretical approach that the depressed person is likely to give up easily and fail to try in future instances due to the factors noted above.

This theory was very popular in the mid 1970s. However, it has not retained its popularity, probably for at least two reasons. First, constant reformulation was necessary because of flaws within the theory. This problem led to various theoretical modifications, and thus, confusion about the most recent version. Second, there has never been a close relationship established between this causative theory and treatment of depression. While this may not be essential in every instance, it most certainly is an advantage for a given theoretical approach. This theory and the previously discussed psychological formulation depend heavily on whether internal or external events are perceived as primary factors which the person "attributes" to a particular outcome. Perceptions or attributions of these events are primary in the extent to which given behaviors are seen as negative and lead to greater degrees of depression. The third psychological theory to be briefly reviewed has a somewhat different bent.

Social Learning Theory

Lewinsohn (1974) hypothesized that a low rate of response-contingent positive reinforcement constitutes a sufficient explanation for many cases of depression. It is explicitly stated in his theory that only unipolar depression can be explained. He assumes that a low rate of response-contingent positive reinforcement acts as an eliciting stimulus for some depressive behaviors including fatigue, lack of interest, and somatic complaints. Lewinsohn (1974) argues that the environment maintains depressive and adaptive behaviors. The depressed person learns to gain considerable social reinforcement in the form of sympathy and attention for his depressive verbal and nonverbal behaviors. This reinforcement maintains and actually exacerbates the problem. The degree to which the individual's behavior is maintained by reinforcement rather than the amount of reinforcement received is assumed to be critical for the occurrence of depression. Lewinsohn contends that the occurrence of behavior followed by positive reinforcement is vital if depression is to be avoided. When an individual's behavior is unlikely to be followed by reinforcement, the behavior decreases or is eliminated. Conversely, the individual will have a decrease in positive, nondepressive behaviors when reinforcement is not present. The cognitive aspects of the person's behavior are also discussed. As reinforcement of particular social responses decreases and the environment becomes less reinforcing, the likelihood of depression increases, causing low self-esteem and feelings of inferiority along with other undesirable feelings.

Environmental causes have been among the most popular explanations, particularly for unipolar depression. However, even for bipolar depression, environmental factors may be important for sustaining or exacerbating symptoms of depression. As noted earlier, there is also some evidence to show that parental behaviors may be associated with depression in children and adolescents (Weissman & Paykel, 1974). It has been observed, for example, that depressed mothers have limited parenting skills such as inhibited affect, greater difficulty showing affection, and problems in communication. And, higher rates of parental depression are observed among children and adolescents who are depressed, evincing not only a genetic but an environmental association (Welner, Welner, McCrary, & Leonard, 1977; Eisenbruch, 1983). In a more recent study it was found that parents of depressed children rewarded their children less than did parents with nondepressed children (Cole & Rehm, 1986). These data suggest differing interaction styles between members of healthy families and those where childhood depression is apparent.

The social effect of depressive behavior with parents and other adults is striking and negative. Mullins, Peterson, Wonderlich, and Reaven (1986) proved this point in their examination of depressed children. Adults were asked to view one of four films in which a child was portrayed as either depressed or not and as having experienced either high or low life stress. Subjects rated their own level of depression, anxiety, and hostility before and after viewing the film. The children viewed had varying levels of depression which consistently influenced almost every rating. Attitudes and views toward the depressed child were in strikingly negative terms. It was assumed by the authors that the depressed child who perceives himself/herself as unwanted, unloved, and rejected may in fact have an undistorted view of reality.

SUMMARY

This chapter presented depression as we currently define it for children and adolescents along with popular notions of etiology. It should be re-emphasized that a major evaluation in the definition of depression among children and adolescents has occurred in a very short period of time. Until recently there was considerable question about the existence of depression in this group, with a good deal of the debate appearing in the professional literature. This issue has been largely resolved with the next issue for discussion being whether various categories, such as masked depression, were valid and helpful. The existence of a number of overt symptoms of childhood depression is now largely accepted. However, researchers currently believe that depression and other forms of psychopathology may coexist and merit further investigation. There is the possibility of overlapping disorders, including depression and conduct disorder, depression, and anxiety, and of other possible combinations. Furthermore, the effects of parental behavior and additional significant others in the environment can and do affect childhood prob lems. This issue is now receiving attention within the area of childhood depression and certainly merits further study, as it has major implications for assessment and treatment.

While much still needs to be done, it would seem that clinicians now have a firm grasp on the causes of childhood depression and how it is exhibited. The next chapter of this book will address methods used to assess these problems in children and adolescents.

Chapter 2

Assessment with Interviews, Direct Observation, and Biological Markers

Assessment is a very important and heavily studied topic in the field of childhood and adolescent depression. For this reason, the practitioner must be familiar with and aware of the most up-to-date and systematic ways of evaluating childhood and adolescent psychopathology. Therefore, this book devotes two chapters to the topic. The first of these chapters reviews interviews, direct observation, and the biological markers that have been developed to assess depression. The second assessment chapter focuses exclusively on checklists, given the large number of available instruments and their importance in diagnosis and evaluation of treatment outcome. These instruments are, at this point, the centerpiece for assessing childhood depression.

The emphasis on assessment procedures as organized and described here is not to suggest that checklists are more important than other methods. Rather, it is a reflection of the great deal of attention given to these assessment techniques in the literature. It is emphasized throughout the assessment chapters that multiple methods, using direct observation, interviewing and reports of parents, teachers, and the children themselves, should be used whenever possible. Thus, the full range of methods to be described should be considered.

FUNCTIONS OF ASSESSMENT

It should be noted that assessment has several important functions. One is obviously to diagnose persons. In addition, it is important to determine if the individual meets criteria for depression. However, assessment should also serve other functions.

The second primary assessment goal is evaluation of treatment outcome. In Figures 2-1 and 2-2, two options are presented for assessing treatment effectiveness. Figure 2-1 is a pictoral representation of test administration prior to treatment and after a diagnosis of depression has been made. After the patient and therapist conclude that optimal gains have occurred, a posttest evaluation is made, typically after many weeks (e.g., 15) or a few months (4 to 6). This assessment allows for a direct comparison of factor scores on specific behaviors and overall or total scores on depressive symptoms. Also, since norms are typically available if checklists are used, the therapist may also be able to draw some general conclusions about the severity of the client's symptoms at pretest and posttest when compared to other children.

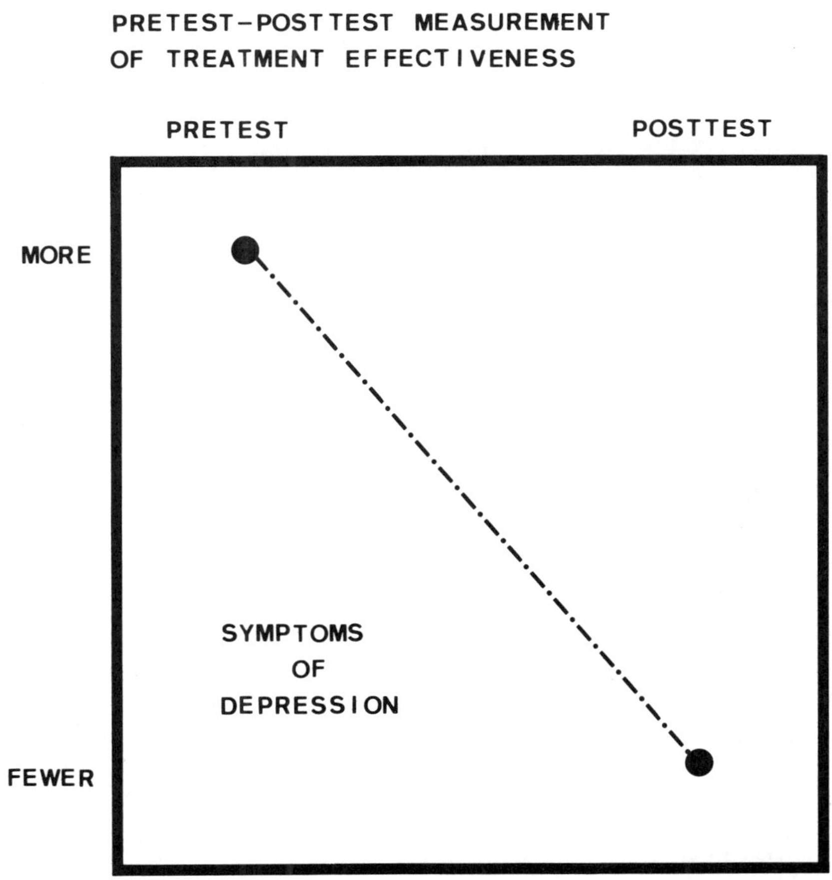

FIGURE 2-1. Traditional pretest-posttest evaluation of treatment effectiveness. Severity of the problem before and after treatment is measured at only one point in time for each.

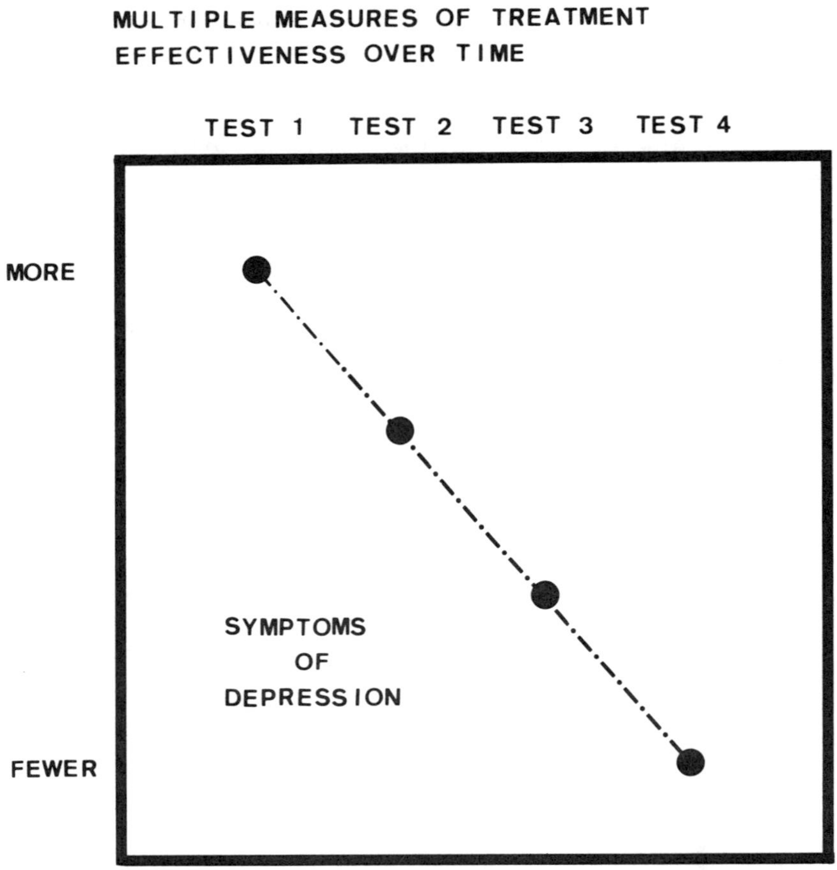

FIGURE 2–2. Pretest and posttest data are collected along with measures of treatment effectiveness at other points in time. Trends in change may be determined more specifically across time. Determining the pattern of change may prove to be of considerable importance for treatment decisions.

A similar approach is taken in Figure 2-2. However, the intervals between assessments may be shorter, typically two to four weeks. The behaviors evaluated need to be more discrete than with the pretest-posttest evaluations. Thus, for example, one may wish to develop homework assignments for initiating social interactions with others if no major improvements are noted. Means of reinforcing these responses and role playing specific examples of when and how this might be accomplished are also likely to be reviewed. *The same measures are often of differing but equal utility for meeting these two diverse goals, a point to which the reader should take careful note*. Those measures that will be most useful for various goals are mentioned throughout the remainder of this book.

The next issue addressed is points to consider in assessment, then various interview techniques, followed by a review of direct observational methods and, lastly, a review of biological assessment techniques.

POINTS TO CONSIDER IN ASSESSMENT

Interviews and checklists have proven to be important methods of evaluating depression in children. And several factors should be considered in their use to ensure maximum benefit. One point to consider is the child's age. Younger children and those with special problems (i.e., hyperactivity) will have shorter attention spans than other children tested. Thus, fewer and shorter measures (in time needed for administration) should be a consideration relative to other childhood problems. Also, the amount of time needed to complete an assessment instrument will likely be greater. Items may need to be read and reread to the children, paraphrasing, giving examples, and having the child repeat back what was said. Adaptive devices such as pictorial representations of topics may be needed or human figures or drawings can be useful aids in getting across various ideas. These strategies may be necessary to ensure understanding by little ones. Two or three, 20- to 40-item scales would probably be a minimum assessment package and as a rule 15 to 20 minutes of testing at a sitting may be best. The examiner may wish to break up the assessment sessions with play periods incorporating a parent.

A second consideration is the comfort and motivation of the child during testing. It may be necessary to have a parent present in the testing room for emotional support and to help the tester identify and clarify when the child is or is not having difficulty understanding what is being asked. Making the environment as pleasant as possible for the child can also be an asset. For example, the experimenter or clinician may allow the child to pick a toy to play with for doing a good job on the test and/or provide the child with gum, candy, or other small rewards for paying attention and answering the questions. These procedures can help rapport and ensure the accuracy of responses.

A third issue involves parent(s). Typically the mother will be the parent who brings the child to the clinic. However, whether it be parent, grandparent, or whomever, several issues need to be considered. What, for example, is the adult's reading level? In some instances,it may be necessary to read items to the parent when checklist information on the child is needed. Similarly, there may be instances when the parent cannot understand what is being requested on a particular item or via the instructions. It is recommended that the tester ask the parent to explain what is expected as a means of assuring that an acceptable level of comprehension has been achieved. If possible, both parents should be interviewed independently. These data can be compared, or in some cases, averaging parent responses can be used and may be of considerable benefit in attaining more representative information.

The teacher is another person from whom information may be needed. However, for the psychologist, psychiatrist, or other health professional who works outside the school system, it may be difficult to obtain this information due to the many commitments of the teacher's time. If the parents can talk directly with the teacher, it can often enhance the likelihood of obtaining the necessary information. Similarly, if there is a school psychologist in the system familiar with depression assessment who can assist by explaining the assessment instruments to the teacher, considerable benefit in accuracy of information and support for the overall assessment is likely to result. These points can be included in the clinical interview.

CLINICAL INTERVIEW

Discussing symptomatology with a client in an open-ended format is undoubtedly the oldest form of assessment and still, easily, the most widely used in applied, nonuniversity-based settings. Based on the theoretical orientation of the clinician, some or a considerable degree of variability in the content and format of the interview may occur. Needless to say, considerable experience is needed to carry out such an endeavor successfully, and the complexity of the task is reflected in the considerable literature that has developed around these efforts (e.g., MacKinnon & Michels, 1971). As entire books have been written on the topic, it would not be possible to give an exhaustive account of this issue here. However, several common features and issues to consider in such evaluations are briefly presented.

One important issue, particularly with children, is development. Cognitive abilities, response to stress, age at onset, and varying patterns of symptomatology are extremely important variables to be aware of (Campbell, 1983). This issue has only recently begun to receive extensive attention from the research community, but it is of obvious importance to practitioners. It was mentioned earlier, for example, that symptoms such as crying frequently would constitute relatively normal behavior for a two-year-old but certainly not for older children (e.g., 12 years of age). Vocabulary is another issue. It has been this writer's experience that many of the checklists and particularly the structured interviews may overestimate many young children's facility with vocabulary. If a number of words cannot be understood, frustration with the interview and inaccurate information is likely to result. The only way to determine the appropriateness of various terminology is to obtain information on the child's reading level and, through direct questioning of parents, teacher, and the children, about potentially problematic vocabulary before beginning the interview. The interviewer should feel free, however, to stop the interview at any point if it becomes apparent that the information being obtained is incomplete or inaccurate based on issues such as those noted above.

With depression, and many other forms of psychopathology for that matter, an important variable is the course of the disorder. Obtaining this information can often be difficult at best. For those readers who have asked parents about their children's developmental milestones, the well-meant but often grossly inaccurate reports that are provided point up the difficulty of obtaining reliable information within this domain. Similarly, young children often have difficulty with the concept of time. They may not be able to adequately or accurately portray their symptoms from even one or two days prior to the interview, let alone the two to three weeks that are often needed with measures of depression or general psychopathology. Some strategies for dealing with this issue might include obtaining information from several other sources such as parents, teachers, and health professionals. Where possible it is also advisable to retest/reinterview the child in two to three weeks to enhance reliability.

The interview itself would typically be oriented toward generating the information necessary for making a DSM-III-R diagnosis. Initially, the clinician would need to make some effort to put the child at ease. Depending on his/her age, this might include playing some type of game, involving a parent, or talking about various activities with which the child would feel comfortable. A reward of some sort such as candy, soda, or other tangible or social reinforcers has been something this writer has typically mentioned early in the interview. The child is told that he or she can earn rewards for answering questions honestly and to the fullest extent possible. Also, a standard procedure is to inform the child as to the reason for seeing the clinician and to stress that the goal will be helping the child feel better. Assuming the ice can be adequately broken, the remainder of the session should be devoted to the type of questioning needed to *obtain or refute* a DSM-III-R diagnosis.

The Unstructured Interview

When employing the unstructured interview, one approach has been to use open-ended questions. This format which is based largely on humanistic approaches to treatment and assessment relies on allowing the child sufficient freedom to guide the interviewer into various topics of conversation. An advantage that some feel this approach has is the opportunity to explore the widest range of topic areas possible (Palmer, 1983). Palmer suggests that in one to two hours three major issues can be addressed: (1) The child's view of the complaints, symptoms, and stressors; (2) The child's view of his or her current environment (home, peers, school) and current functioning (sleeping, eating, digestion, and elimination habits, and with an adolescent sexual interests as well as feelings about them); and, (3) The child's view of his or her own development and history, including projections about the future. As the reader may readily determine, the open-ended approach also typically results in more diffuse responses. This method is less likely to result in a diagnosis and most certainly is less likely to result in the identification of specific symptoms that may be of benefit in developing treatment plans with more structured interventions. The focus is much more on the process of treatment than on the specific identification and remediation of observable symptoms. More general goals such as self-awareness, self-actualization and enhanced self-esteem are approached through the common dialogue of the therapist and the child.

Some of the points emphasized in unstructured or less structured interviews have been maintained in more current thinking about the evaluation process. Descriptions of everyday life events at school and home employing concrete examples are particularly relevant. Often this may be followed with a detailed description of daily events, complaints, and problem areas. Identification of antecedents (what happens immediately before the problem erupts) and consequences (what happens immediately after the problem) are typically discussed in detail with the hope of pinpointing behaviors that might later be changed. A second advantage of this approach is the description of family interactions, school routine, play activities, eating habits, study habits, and other behaviors which would, at least to some degree, exemplify the person's habits as they might apply to depression. One could argue that such information could be obtained in a more systematic fashion through a more structured approach. However, in a less structured format, it is most likely the case that information could be better stated in the child's own words and there would probably be decreased risk of the child being led by the interviewer to certain conclusions. The child's own chronology of events could more accurately be represented. Despite these potential advantages, however, the trend would appear to be toward a more highly structured means of obtaining information from children, their parents, and important others such as teachers. The most common of these approaches have been structured interviews which are briefly reviewed next. Checklists are the topic of the next chapter.

The Structured Interview

There are some problems with the open-ended interview, since little consistency exists across raters and even within the same rater. Interviewers may forget or overlook particular items. And, while this method does remain popular, it is also the case that structured interviews have become increasing popular. It is unlikely that the structured interview will ever take the place of the open-ended interview. Nonetheless, it seems to be developing as one important method of interviewing. These instruments are extensive and particularly comprehensive relative to checklists or other assessment methods. Each of these measures is reviewed below.

It has been pointed out that the growing recognition of identifiable symptoms has led to increased conversation with children, as opposed to playing with them, as a means of assessment (Puig-Antich, Chambers, & Tabrizi, 1983). Additionally, it may be anxiety producing for a child to play with a strange adult in unusual surroundings and much of the information obtained through play may have no relevance to treatment. The time needed to accommodate the new situation may be considerable, thus further minimizing the popularity of play as a primary interview technique. Because of these problems, professionals have turned to other means of assessment. Herjanic and Campbell (1975), for example, demonstrated that self-report checklists and structured interviews are reliable means of obtaining data from children. It is probably fair to say that the popularity of this approach is increasing.

Based on the theoretical orientation of the clinician, the content of the interview may differ. A recent trend that this writer strongly supports is emphasis on objective, observable phenomenon such as a loss of weight, the tendency to cry easily and other observable behavior. This approach will result in more accurate material of higher reliability, which is devoid of specific philosophy. This approach can include self-generated historical material and information that can be tied to checklists. A second approach, which is both more comprehensive and more time consuming, is to employ a structured interview with (preferably) or without checklists. The standard measure of this type for potentially depressed young persons is the Kiddie-SADS. While this measure is the most visible of the structured interviews, it is not in use in most applied settings. Perhaps as the area of childhood depression becomes more widely accepted as an important one needing attention from the mental health community, increased popularity of structured interviews may result.

Kiddie-SADS Interview

The major interview currently in use as previously noted, according to Rehm et al. (1987), is the Kiddie-SADS-P (Puig-Antich & Chambers,

1978). This measure was originally developed for evaluating major depression in prepuberty. It, much like the Child Depression Inventory which is discussed in the next chapter, is a child version of an adult scale, the Schedule for Affective Disorders and Schizophrenia (SADS) (Endicott & Spitzer, 1978). It is used with children 6 to 17 years of age for the diagnosis of depression with either RDC or DSM-III-R criteria. (The reader may recall that the DSM-III-R criteria was developed from the RDC.) Thus, they are very similar. Four major categories of child and adolescent problems are assessed including affect, anxiety, conduct, and psychosis. A major strength of this scale is that it has been designed so that both the child and parent can be interviewed to enhance the reliability of the assessment. The Kiddie-SADS-P is a structured diagnosis-interview that focuses on the emotional status of the child at the present time, defined as the point at which assessment is being conducted (Puig-Antich & Chambers, 1978). Both past and present episodes are evaluated, and it is used strictly as a diagnostic instrument. Diagnoses that can be arrived at are minor depression, major depression, mania, hypomania, schizophrenia, schizoaffective disorder, autism, anorexia nervosa, attention deficit disorder, conduct disorder, separation anxiety, panic disorder, phobias, obsessive compulsive disorder, overanxiousness, alcohol use, drug abuse, and suicide.

The interview of the parent (the child is also evaluated) begins with an unstructured overview of the specifics involved in the present episode, including onset, duration, and a description of all presenting problems. Then, the interviewer proceeds to the structured components of the evaluation (which is by far the largest part of the overall assessment), including a review of salient symptoms of most child psychiatric problems.

A branching tree of questions is provided for each diagnosis. Initial screening with a few items in various content areas tends to be sufficient to rule out a given diagnosis, thus sparing the interviewer and child an extensive question-and-answer phase for diagnoses that are not relevant. Items are scored *no information, yes* or *no*. For some responses there may be up to seven possible categories in a Likert format (e.g., 0 = No information, 1 = never hospitalized, 2 = less than 3 months, 4 = less than 1 year, 5 = less than 2 years, 6 = less than 5 years, and 7 = 5 or more years, for an item making reference to the course of the disorder). The clinician first interviews a parent (typically the mother) recording responses on a precoded scoring form. Next, the child is interviewed using the same procedure. It is stated that differences between parent and child scores are resolved during the interview. This writer has some concern about this approach, since leading the client to a given answer may occur. A more systematic method might be to average the parent and child ratings.

Test-retest reliability with 52 children, ages 6 to 17,who had been referred to an outpatient clinic indicated that depression and conduct disorder and related symptoms could be assessed reliably. Reliability, while good—at least for depression—was not as positive as data obtained using the SADS with adults.

These summary ratings are used to make the final diagnosis. The decision is based on the "clinical judgment" of the rater. The authors of the scale caution that a good deal of experience in general interviewing and specific training in the administration of the Kiddie-SADS-P is needed. This training is available only from the developers of the scale and thus would be expensive and difficult to obtain.

This measure has some demonstrated reliability although it has not been researched to the same degree as the checklists discussed in the following chapter (Hirsch, Paez, Chambers, Davis, & Puig-Antich, 1980).

There are other structured interviews but these typically deal with general psychopathology and are not specific to depression. The NIMH Interview Schedule for Children (DISC) (Costello, Edelbrock, Dulcan, & Kalas, 1984) is perhaps the best known of these. The point is that measures such as this one, which has been supported with NIMH funding, are likely to prove to be a beneficial means of enhancing the reliability of diagnoses. The DISC provides DSM-III diagnoses for person 6 to 17 years of age. As with the Kiddie-SADS there are parent (DISC-P) and child (DISC-C) versions of the scale and they can be administered by clinicians or paraprofessionals trained specifically in the administration of the scale. Questions include functioning and activity at school, peer relationships, home relationships, and community life. There is also a computer program that picks out different information for making particular diagnoses. The measures takes 45 to 60 minutes to complete for parent or child versions. Symptoms can be reported reliably, although parent interviews appear to be better methods of discriminating between diagnoses than child reports. This interview method may be particularly useful for the child who has not previously been evaluated, therefore making it difficult to narrow the assessment to depression or the other few disorders measured on the Kiddie-SADS.

A case for the measurement of general psychopathology could also be made with the DICA. This instrument is another measure of general psychopathology for use with children and adolescents. The DICA is based on DSM-III and is used with children 6 to 17 years of age (Herjanic & Campbell, 1977). The measure, typically administered by a trained female interviewer, takes 60 to 90 minutes to complete. There are three phases to the scale. Initially, a joint interview is performed with the parent and child in order to obtain relevant chronological information about the person and his other problem. The parent (mother in most cases) and the child are then interviewed separately. Similar questions are presented to cover 18 DSM-III diagnostic categories. The final phase includes only the mother and involves a review of information about developmental and medical history and other possible psychiatric diagnoses not reviewed with the child. Data have yet to appear on this instrument. However, based on the other two structured interviews, it is likely that reliability on diagnoses would be considerably higher than what is found using only the open-ended interview.

DIRECT OBSERVATION

The approach that involves identifying a few discrete behaviors and observing them in the child's learning setting has received very little attention. This approach would seem to have considerable promise, though, and is in a much different domain than the other assessment measures. For this latter reason it is a method of assessment that should be employed where practical.

Direct observational methods have been described in considerable detail by others. Therefore,the reader is referred elsewhere for a detailed description of these methods (Frame & Matson, 1987). However, the clinician should operationally define the behaviors, establish independent reliability assessments of the target behavior and take Likert ratings or frequency counts of the target behaviors on some systematic schedule, preferably with data collected in the natural environment. Several studies have focused on specific aspects of depressed verbal behavior as targets for modification via psychological interventions. Robinson and Lewinsohn (1973), for example, identified a slowed rate of speech as a depressive target behavior in a chronically depressed psychiatric patient. Number of words per 30-second interval was tabulated with a hand counter by an observer who was stationed behind a one-way mirror. Rate of speech, the characteristic of depression studied, was effectively modified, indicating that this system can prove to be sensitive as a means of evaluating treatment outcome. Since many characteristics of depression involve overt behaviors such as diminshed social and motor activity, sad facial expression, and slow speech, direct observation should be appropriate.

Kazdin, Esveldt-Dawson, Sherick, and Colbus (1985) tested 62 inpatient children 8 to 13 years of age. Observations were made during a daily free-play period that occurred routinely on the unit before lunch. During a 30-minute period, half the children went off the unit for lunch and when they returned, the remainder of the children went to eat. Observations were made of those children who were not at lunch. During this free period, children could play in an activity area or the TV room. In the activity area were games, play materials, and group activities. Staff supervision was available to intervene if disruptive or dangerous behavior occurred. Observations were made between the second and fourth weeks of hospitalization for five consecutive weekdays. As the authors pointed out, children needed a period of time to accommodate to their surroundings as a way of ensuring that a typical sample of behavior could be obtained.

Behaviors for observation were selected based on DSM-III criteria and observational studies that had been conducted with adults (Williams, Barlow, & Agras, 1972). These items were selected for intervention based on responses the children had made previously. Behaviors in three categories were examined and are listed below. The responses and categories are those the clinician may wish to consider for inclusion in the evaluation and treatment of depressed children.

1. *Social Activity.* Four behaviors were included: (a) *Talking* was defined as verbally interacting with another child when there was an exchange of comments or ongoing dialogue. Single unanswered questions were not scored. (b) *Playing a game* was defined as participating in a game, such as a board game with one or more individuals. (c) *Participating in a group activity* was defined as engaging in behavior with a group of individuals not necessarily involved in a structured game; interacting with a group, taking turns, looking at materials together, working together on a special task. (d) *Interacting with staff* included contacting staff members, either conversing or playing with staff.

2. *Solitary behavior.* Five behaviors were included: (a) *Playing a game alone* referred to engaging in a game activity (board game, cards or tasks with play materials) by oneself. (b) *Working on an academic task* involved reading, studying, or writing by oneself. (c) *Listening and watching* involved looking, listening, and reacting to a TV program or radio or music by oneself. (d) *Straightening one's room* involved putting one's belongings in the proper place or cleaning one's room. (e) *Grooming* included engaging in behaviors related to self-care such as getting dressed or changing clothes, grooming, and bathing.

3. *Affect-related expression.* Four responses were included: (a) *Smiling* involved using facial muscles to upturn the corners of the mouth and/or facial expressions of joy or pleasure. (b) *Frowning* was the lowering of one's eyebrows or downward turning of the mouth and/or facial expressions of displeasure. (c) *Arguing* was defined as tense, emotional, verbal interactions including loud voice, shouting, losing one's temper, or displaying outbursts of anger. (d) *Complaining*, the final behavior evaluated, included verbal expressions of unhappiness, dissatisfaction, or pain.

These target behaviors are listed since they may serve as a model for the clinician interested in using direct observations of depression. As noted, this approach may be worth considering in combination with other methods as a means of evaluation.

The reader can see that the responses selected were overt and observable, thus decreasing the amount of subjective interpretation in the assessment. A list of discrete behaviors such as this is much more likely to be sensitive to changes produced by treatment than any other assessments developed to this point. As a result, this approach may serve particularly well as a means of evaluating treatment outcome as discussed earlier in this chapter. Direct observation might also prove useful for a pretest-posttest evaluation or for periodic multiple assessment trials. Lowered social activity and affect-related expression have been shown to correlate highly with diagnoses of depression. However, self-report data on the CDI and BID-R did not show as strong a relation. The authors of this study suggest that different dimensions of depressive phenomenon might be evaluated with these various measures, since multiple measures in at least two domains were highly correlated. Given that depression assessment in children is still in a developing state, this appears to be the most conservative hypothesis. The best motto at this time would seem to be to cast a broad net with respect to the number and type of assessment measures used.

Another consideration should be the development of procedures to make the direct observation standardized. Several developments in this regard have occurred in specific assessments of family interactions. Games or activities designed for family members to engage in while being observed through a one-way mirror at the clinic by the therapist could be considered. At this point, no standardized system exists for such an approach. Obviously,however, the content that elicits depressive symptoms, if present, should be considered.

Libet, Lewinsohn, and Javorek (1973) provide another possible approach by describing ratings for groups of patients in a mental health setting and ratings in a home setting. They evaluated a variety of behaviors including the display of fewer questions and verbal responses. The depressed adults who were studied were also affected more by aversive reactions and elicited fewer positive reactions. These individuals were also more silent, slower to respond to reactions, and elicited a lower rate of positive reinforcement. Additional problem areas identified in other studies using these coding methods for depressed adults have included low activity level in the family (Lewinsohn, Weinstein, & Alper, 1970), few family initiations to the client, and negative reactions from the spouse (Lewinsohn & Shaffer, 1971), as well as low rates of mutual reinforcement (Lewinsohn & Shaw, 1969). Home observations as a basis for assessment also provide advantages for subsequent therapy interventions by providing data that can be used as objective feedback to clients. Also, home observations focus attention on the interpersonal behavior of the client and his or her family. Any time observations can be done in the natural environment a much clearer picture of the problem can be formed.

The problem with home observations is that they can be very costly and often quite complex. As a result, a less sophisticated system may sometimes be more practical. Fuchs and Rehm (1977) provide one example of a procedure of this type. They used 10-minute videotaped segments of interactions among groups of clients with the therapist absent. The number of statements made in 10 minutes was counted as a simple assessment of verbal activity level. These authors and others have rated behaviors such as direct references to people, expressions of feelings, nonpersonal references, speech rate, eye contact, and duration of gaze toward another.

There are also some generic interaction coding systems designed for the family that the reader may wish to consider. Atkeson and Forehand (1981) recommend clinic observations of children for two reasons: first, potential difficulties in family interactions may be easily identified; and second, the standard situations that the therapist can create within and between client comparisons. While these systems have typically been used for conduct problems, they would also seem to have considerable merit for evaluating the problems regarding interactions that are so common in depressed children and adolescents. For small children, a program that employs toys and games can be used. For older children and youth, structured tasks requiring family participation and interactions may be considered. Observations can then be made unobtrusively through a one-way mirror and specific discrete target responses, such as those mentioned earlier in this section, or direct observation, can be rated and scored.

In one system of this type, parents are given instructions prior to the rating period (Forehand & Peed, 1979). Each parent is instructed to interact with his or her child in two contexts, the Child's Game and the Parent's Game. The parent is instructed to engage in any activity the child chooses in the Child's Game, allowing the child to determine the nature and rules of the interaction. The Child's Game, then, is essentially a free play situation. In the Parent's Game, the parent is required to engage the child in activities whose rules and nature are determined by the parent, producing essentially a command situation. A coding period of 5 to 10 minutes for the parent and child periods is used. The amount of time may need to be varied somewhat, however, with depressed persons. Several specific behaviors are evaluated for the parent and child and are as follows:

Coding Parent Behavior

1. *Rewards.* These behaviors included praise, approval, or positive physical attention that refers to the child or to the child's activities. Verbal rewards include both specific (labeled) and nonspecific (unlabeled) reference to praiseworthy behavior.

2. *Attends.* This is a descriptive word that follows and refers to (a) the child's ongoing behavior, (b) objects directly related to the child's play, (c) his or her spatial position (e.g., you're standing in the middle of the room), or (d) his or her appearance.

3. *Questions:* These are interrogatives to which the only appropriate response is verbal.

4. *Commands.* (a) Alpha commands are orders, rules, suggestions, or questions to which a motor response is appropriate and feasible. (b) Beta commands do not allow the child the opportunity to demonstrate compliance. Beta commands include parental commands that are vague to the point that child compliance cannot be determined, that are interrupted by further parental talk before the child has the opportunity to comply, or that are carried out by the parent before an opportunity to comply occurs.

5. *Warnings.* These statements describe aversive consequences to be delivered by the parent if the child fails to comply with a parental command.

6. *Time-out.* This method is used by the parent and is clearly intended to remove the child from positive reinforcement due to inappropriate behavior.

Coding Child Behavior

1. *Child compliance.* This is an appropriate motor response initiated within five seconds of a parental alpha command.

2. *Child noncompliance.* Same as above except beta commands may be present.

3. *Child inappropriate behavior.* Whining, crying, yelling, tantrums, aggression, and various inappropriate statements.

The reader is encouraged to employ some of these points when developing an observational rating system for child and adolescent depression. While many of the responses in the Forehand system, particularly with regard to child behaviors, do not correspond to depression, the system would appear to be applicable with some modification.

The general form of direct behavioral observation is a flexible system that should be part of the assessment battery in almost every case.

BIOCHEMICAL AND PHYSIOLOGICAL MEASURES

The final area of review in this chapter is biological markers, first pioneered with adults. These assessments are divided into two groups. They include chemical measures of bodily substances (wet measures) and measures of muscle tension (dry measures). These techniques have not caught on in any large way as yet, probably because of the expense associated with buying the necessary equipment for making such assessments. Additionally, a considerable number of adaptations of the techniques devised for adults would be needed for implementation with children. However, measures such as these might prove to be one of the more useful approaches with children, since lack of or limited verbal skills are often evident. And in such cases the most common forms of assessment, interview, and self-report information might be difficult to obtain and/or the information may not prove to be particularly comprehensive.

Biochemical Measures

Among the biochemical measures, those pioneered with depressed adults that were found to have some utility include the dexamethasone suppression test (DST), MHPG, and growth hormone secretion. Each of these three approaches is discussed briefly.

The DST test has proven useful in may instances, although the results are not always precise. It is an accurate marker of depression only in approximately 25% to 60% of the cases (Carroll, 1982). Cortisol levels are not suppressed when the person is given dexamethasone if depression is present. If the person is not depressed cortisol levels are depressed. For the last 10 years, this measure has been a widely used clinical and research tool for evaluating major affective disorders (Peselow, Baxter, Fieve, & Barouche, 1987). Failure to suppress on the DST has been reported for children and adolescents in both inpatient and outpatient settings (Extein, Rosenberg, Pottash, & Gold, 1982; Geller, Rogel, &

Knitter, 1983; Livingston, Reis, & Ringdahl, 1984). Thus, this depression measure would seem to have some utility although the method is far from foolproof. It is suggested that this measure be considered as an adjunct rather than as a primary measure of depression. Additionally, it is recommended for use only when it is one of several measures employed.

Considerable development of more specific biochemical assays for depression are likely in the future. Other types of assays, which will result in more precise and accurate measurement, are probable although time, expense, and availability of labs to evaluate blood samples is likely to be a problem in many settings. To date not a great deal of research has been done in this regard. And, while the DST test may not be satisfactory in many instances, and further study on this and related measures is warranted. The next approach reviewed, physiological methods, may also hold promise.

Physiological measures

There is a sizable literature on general muscle tension as a symptom indicative of depressed patients (Whatmore & Kohli, 1968). As a result, some efforts at evaluating affect specific to facial muscle tension have come forth. The notion of examining specific muscle patterns has proven useful in differentiating between affective disorders and other conditions in some research with adults and would be aided by physiological measurement because these muscle patterns are not readily identifiable by the untrained eye. The corrugator muscle has proven to be one of the most sensitive areas for measuring positive versus negative affective imagery. Depressed adults showed attenuation of facial EMG patterns associated with happy imagery, and marginal accentuation of facial EMG patterns with sad imagery (Schwartz, Fair, Salt, Mandel, & Klerman, 1976a, 1976b). Additionally, persons tested while depressed and then again after effective treatment reduced depression showed this to be an effective measure for evaluating treatment outcome (Schwartz, Fair, Mandel, Salt, Mieske, & Klerman, 1978).

Unfortunately, pilot data with children has not been as useful. In work the writer was involved in at the University of Pittsburgh School of Medicine, the informal finding was that the smaller facial features and facial muscles of children made it difficult to replicate the results found with adults. No controlled studies with children have been done to date, perhaps for these and other reasons. However, physiological methods may yet prove to be effective and certainly deserve further study. Should a developmental factor prove to be significant, it would still be of value for researchers and clinicians to know the age level at which EMG and other physiological measures would be of benefit. This issue is yet to be resolved and at this point *accurate and reliable* physiological measures of depression with children simply do not exist.

SUMMARY

The interview, long the staple of the clinician is still perhaps the most common means of acquiring information for diagnostic purposes. However, the development of structured interviews, biochemical measures, and checklists that are described in the next chapter, indicate that most researchers now believe the interview alone is insufficient as a means of making diagnoses and treatment decisions for depression in younger persons. The emphasis at present is on developing more systematic and structured ways of collecting information while at the same time allowing for sufficient latitude for additional questioning on information that is not covered by the predeveloped checklists and other structured evaluation methods.

The structured interview became quite popular in the mid-1970s, with the evaluation of several general psychopathology methods and one specific to depression and other severe forms of psychopathology. These procedures have, however, decreased in popularity. The problem has been the extreme length and considerable amount of training needed to complete interviews. Shorter versions with language that is easier to understand will likely appear in the next few years and may perhaps enjoy more broad-based use. It is this writer's view that such developments will be necessary to ensure widespread acceptance of these procedures.

Physiological and biochemical measures show some promise. However, they are not at this point ready for common use in the clinical setting. These measures may eventually be a beneficial adjunct to the methods already available. At present, however, checklists are the most viable of the systematic assessment methods. A detailed review of these methods is provided in the next chapter.

Chapter 3

Assessment with Checklists

In the previous chapter, some methods of assessing depression in children were evaluated. Given the volume of information that has been written on checklists, a separate chapter is being devoted exclusively to this topic, which is the hallmark and centerpiece for assessing childhood depression. This chapter will begin with a rationale of some of the most important reasons why checklists are used, followed by a description of specific assessment methods. The final section of the chapter is a general summary of assessment issues.

Checklists have easily been the most extensively studied and used methods to diagnose depression in children and adolescents. While this approach or any other assessment method should not be used alone, there are some good reasons for the popularity of this particular method. First, these procedures can be administered rapidly, a constant concern for most clinicians due to time constraints. Second, a standardized list of items gives a uniform comparison across individuals. Third, normative data are available often with cutoff scores for depression, thus taking some of the subjectivity and guesswork out of diagnosis. Fourth, one can obtain data from direct care staff and mental health professionals best acquainted with the client. Fifth, depression scales, unlike interviews or direct behavioral observations, are based on the last two or three weeks of the person's behavior rather than on discrete, brief periods of time, as with the former measures. Sixth and finally, the cost of the evaluation does not appear to be as prohibitive as many other assessment methods because they can be filled out by direct-care staff, parents,or the child himself/herself. It is worth reiterating this point since practical consideration in the typical mental health center, perhaps more than any other factor, determines the utility of a given approach to assessment.

There is also a negative side to these assessment methods. Unlike direct observation, in particular, the reliability of the checklist format seems to be much lower even though a greater range of symptoms is usually tested. Along these same lines, the checklists developed to date have not proven to be good measures of treatment outcome, often not being sufficiently sensitive to adequately evaluate improvements in the depressed individual's behavior. Even with these negative points, however, there are sufficient reasons (as noted earlier) to make this method a useful basis for assessing childhood and adolescent depression. All the available scales cannot be extensively reviewed in this volume. However, some of the more pertinent measures will be discussed.

DIRECT TEST OF CHILD

Several measures can be used as a direct evaluation of the child via self-report and often times can also be evaluated by others. The discussion will begin with a review of the most popular of these assessment procedures, the Child Depression Inventory (CDI) (Kazdin, 1981). This review will be followed by a discussion of the Reynolds Adolescent Depression Scale, Child Depression Scale, Chlidren's Depression Rating Scale, Children's Depression Adjective Checklist, Peer Nomination Inventory for Depression (PNID), Short Children's Depression Inventory, and Depression Self-Rating Scale.

Child Depression Inventory (CDI)

The CDI is the most popular of the child depression checklists. Therefore, it warrants detailed discussion. As with the other measures to be discussed in this section it can be completed quickly, generally in 10 to 20 minutes. There have been three major revisions and several minor revisions of the CDI. The most drastic modifications have encompassed changes of the item format from four to three choices on items. This revision was based partly on examination of the frequency distribution of CDI item choices from 125 normal Canadian school children, plus 39 child guidance youngsters, and 20 normal youngsters in Philadelphia. A three-item choice method was finally selected. Another revision involved random selection of approximately half the items, which were then rearranged so that the first choice evinced the greatest pathology and vice versa for the remaining items. This approach is a safeguard to random responding by the child, which could markedly bias diagnostic information.

The CDI is based on an adult measure, the Beck Depression Inventory (Kovacs & Beck, 1977). It has been used primarily with children ranging in age from 7 to 17. A short form of 12 items is also available (Carlson & Cantwell, 1980). The scale can be filled out quickly since there are only

27 items, each consisting of 3 Likert responses scored as 0, 1, or 2 based on the response chosen by the rater and can be easily administered in 10 to 20 minutes (Saylor, Finch, Spirito, & Bennett, 1984).

It has been recommended that the CDI cut-off scores be interpreted cautiously because the scale is not considered highly accurate as a diagnostic measure of depression (Kovacs, 1983). This situation should not be considered particularly surprising, however, since depressive symptoms are not unique to depressive disorders, and since no one instrument is foolproof. The scale developer's remarks correspond to previous comments made in this book. That is, any well-conducted assessment of childhood depression should include data derived from several sources.

The clinician administering the CDI should first become familiar with the scale by reading over the test and manual carefully. Additionally, those persons who have the time to do so may wish to read studies that tested the scale to gain a better grasp of the measure's strengths and weaknesses (e.g., see Kovacs, 1985). Also, it is recommended that the clinician consider other instruments and formats to employ in determining a battery of methods for diagnosis, evaluating treatment outcome, or other related purposes. The evaluator may wish to employ a two-step process, an initial set of measures which would constitute a general exploratory battery, followed by a second assessment battery whose type and focus would be determined by initial findings. Issues that the clinician might wish to consider include the child's age, expressive and receptive language skills, and severity and intensity of presenting symptoms.

The most common use of the CDI is as a third-party informant measure. However, a self-report form is also available and should be used where possible along with informant ratings. It should be cautioned, however, that for self-report measures, the child may be unwilling or unable to provide the desired information due to cognitive limitations, serious emotional problems, or other reasons (Shoemaker, Erickson, & Finch, 1986). This process would also seem applicable for the other measures to be reviewed in this chapter.

There has been a good deal of research to support the efficacy of the CDI. It has, for example, been found to be a stable indicator of depression over time (Kovacs, 1981) and correlates highly with clinician ratings of depression (Kovacs, Betof, Celebre, Mansheim, Petty, & Raynak, 1977). Additionally, high internal consistency has been established (Orvaschel, Sholomskas, & Weissman, 1980). More recently, the CDI has been factor analyzed. Four subdomains emerged from these analyses (Helsel & Matson, 1984). The items for each of these factors are presented in Table 3-1.

The CDI has been normed primarily on randomly selected school-age

Table 3–1. Factors by item with factor loadings for the Child Depression Inventory (CDI)

Items number	Item name	Factor loadings
Factor 1:	Affective Behavior	
2	Nothing will ever work out for him/her.	(0.35)
3	(S)he does everything wrong.	(0.36)
10	(S)he feels like crying every day.	(0.42)
11	Things bother him/her all the time.	(0.49)
13	(S)he cannot make up his/her mind about things.	(0.49)
15	(S)he has to push him/herself all the time to do school work.	(0.50)
16	(S)he has trouble sleeping every night.	(0.35)
17	(S)he is tired all the time.	(0.41)
18	Most days (s)he does not feel like eating.	(0.35)
23	(S)he does very badly in subjects (s)he used to do well in.	(0.45)
Factor 2:	Image Ideation	
1	(S)he is sad all the time.	(0.55)
6	(S)he is sure that terrible things will happen to him/her.	(0.42)
7	(S)he hates him/herself.	(0.65)
9	(S)he wants to kill him/herself.	(0.32)
14	(S)he looks ugly.	(0.42)
19	(S)he worries about aches and pains all the time.	(0.28)
Factor 3:	Interpersonal Relations	
4	Nothing is fun at all.	(0.65)
12	(S)he does not want to be with people at all.	(0.56)
20	(S)he feels alone all the time.	(0.48)
21	(S)he never has fun at school.	(0.47)
22	(S)he does not have any friends.	(0.51)
24	(S)he can never be as good as the other kids.	(0.51)
25	Nobody really loves him/her.	(0.32)
Factor 4:	Guilt Irritability	
5	(S)he is bad all the time.	(0.59)
8	All bad things are his/her fault.	(0.65)
26	(S)he never does what (s)he is told.	(0.52)
27	(S)he gets into fights all the time.	(0.59)

children but has been found to be useful for mentally retarded children as well (Matson, Helsel, & Barrett, in press).

The most extensive normative sample was reported by Finch, Saylor, and Edwards (1985) who tested 1,463 Florida public school children 7 to 16 years of age. Significant but small age and sex differences were found. These data should prove of some clinical value to the practitioner, since two standard deviations above the mean can be used as a cutoff. Scores numerically higher would signify depression. These authors reported a mean of 9.65 with a standard deviation of 7.30. Kovacs reports a mean of 9.27 and a standard deviation of 7.29.

Smucker, Craighead, Craighead, and Green (1986) have also compiled normative data. They studied 1,252 children 8 to 16 years of age (594 males and 658 females). Their mean score was 9.09 with a standard deviation of 7.04, a figure consistent with norms reported in the two samples previously mentioned. The consistency of these data is of considerable importance. It suggests that normative data and cutoff scores for this measure are well established. Additionally, the criterion validity of the scale was established showing diagnoses of depression to be related to higher scores on the CDI (Carlson & Cantwell, 1979; Kovacs, 1983).

The relationship of the CDI to other measures has also been examined recently. Studying a scale in this fashion is a logical progression once a scale has proven reliable and valid for evaluating a particular phenomenon. The purpose of these studies would be descriptive and of value in helping the clinician to understand the parameters of a given disorder. For example, it has been hypothesized that social skills difficulties are common in depressed persons (Lewinsohn, 1974). This speculation has been empirically supported in children by Helsel and Matson (1984). Similarly, anxiety, low self-esteem, somatic complaints, and passivity seem to be important aspects of this phenomenon (Green, 1980; Jacobsen et al., 1983; Kovacs, 1983; Strauss et al., 1984). Given these data and the previous track record of the measure, the reader may wish to consider the CDI.

Reynolds Adolescent Depression Scale (RADS)

The RADS (Reynolds, 1987) is another well-developed scale beginning to receive attention from clinicans and researchers. It is a 30-item, self-report measure designed to test a wide range of depressive symptoms. Items are endorsed on a four-point scale, including *almost never, hardly ever, sometimes,* and *most of the time*.

The measure was normed on 9,000 adolescent and has good reliability, both internally and on test-retest (Reynolds, 1987). The scale is designed as a self-report measure for children 8 to 13 years of age with items keyed to DSM-III and the research literature. Per each item, facial representations ranging from happy to sad accompany the choice gradient. The child puts an *X* over a particular face to demonstrate how he feels. In a recent study, 166 children 8 to 11 years of age were compared on the RADS, CDI, and measures of anxiety and self-esteem (Reynolds, Anderson, & Bartell, 1985). Additionally, teachers provided global ratings of depression and academic performance. The authors concluded that the reliability and validity of both self-report measures supported their use as child depression measures. However, their data on parent report did not prove to be as encouraging because correlations of parent versus other reports was much lower than correlations between teacher and self-report.

The RADS has some data available on mildly mentally retarded children (N = 26). Test-retest reliability of 0.84 over a 6-week interval was obtained. Similarly, recent work with the CDI has produced data with hearing-impaired children. It should be emphasized that handicapped children are an important and often ignored group, deserving of further study. These data would seem to support the efficacy of the RADS. Whether one should use the CDI over the RADS is open to question. Because the measures can be filled out quickly, the clinician may opt to use both. The CDI at this writing is a better-known instrument probably because it was developed at an earlier date and has been discussed more frequently in the experimental literature.

Children's Depression Scale (CDS)

The CDS is another childhood depression measure receiving some attention (Tisher & Lang, 1983). Tisher and Lang began their effort in developing this scale in 1967. The procedures they followed and describe in their attempts to develop an assessment scale for childhood depression are enlightening and may prove useful to clinicians and researchers. They first reviewed the literature to find items that could be categorized as depression. They included affective responses such as sadness and unhappiness, weeping, negative self-concept such as low self-esteem and feelings of inadequacy, decreases in mental productivity and drive including boredom, withdrawal, lack of energy, discontent, low capacity for pleasure, motor retardation, inability to accept help or comfort, psychosomatic problems such as headaches, abdominal pains, and insomnia and other sleep disturbances. Other items, for example preoccupation with death and difficulties with agression, were also included. The authors state that in phrasing the items,the aim was to describe the depressed child's experience in such a way that the child would recognize her or his feelings and attitudes.

The CDS has 66 items, 48 of these describe negative depressive symptoms (e.g., *often I feel I'm not worth much*, *often I feel lonely*) and 18 positive-oriented responses (*I enjoy myself most of the time*). There is an adult form for use with parents, siblings, teachers, and relatives of the child. In the other and self-report form, each of the 66 items is printed on a separate card. Five boxes are provided and are labeled *very wrong, don't know, not sure, right,* and *very right*. Each box has a slit in the top so that the response selected may be dropped into it. The authors suggest that this format ensures that the respondent will focus attention on one item at a time and that he or she is not unduly influenced by earlier items. The details for administering, scoring, and interpreting the scale are available in a manual (Lang & Tisher, 1978) that can be purchased from the Austrialian Council for Educational Research, Radford House, Fredrick Street, Hawthorn, Victoria, 3122, Australia.

The normative data on the CDS includes 96 children, aged 9 to 16 years, 76 mothers, and 54 fathers. The sample was not random, however. Rather, the children all evinced school refusal.

Another interesting development with the CDS was based on a questionnaire sent to 97 clinicans who had used the scale worldwide. Forty people replied. Most respondents had been using the CDS for between 9 and 12 months and the majority used it mainly with children. Among the comments these persons made were: (1) this measure was helpful in encouraging children to talk about things they did not usually express; (2) it was useful for building rapport; and, (3) the use of boxes rather than the typical paper-and-pencil scoring method was a positive development. It proved to be a help for children to understand how they should respond and was also fun for the children. It is important to note that these authors bring up a very important issue. That is, structured materials, when used properly for encouraging and enhancing interactions between the clinican and the child being interviewed, can be a very important adjunct to the assessment process. Interestingly, no age differences were found on symptoms. It should be cautioned that although this scale has a very ingenious scoring format and considerable potential, there is a major limitation. At this writing there have been no large-scale normative studies as with the CDI and RADS.

Establishing diagnostic and treatment evaluation assessment methods across cultures is of utmost importance. The authors of the CDS should be complimented in this regard, as this measure has been translated from English to Japanese and administered to 389 boys and girls 9 to 18 years of age.

The CDS cannot be used to diagnose depression since cutoff scores have not been established. It should be pointed out, however, that the measure may prove to be an important adjunct, particularly when informant or self-report data cannot be obtained because the person being interviewed cannot follow the paper-and-pencil testing format. Obviously, adaptations to other depression measures may also be considered. However, when changes are made, the norms are invalidated and can only be used for general comparison purposes. Diagnoses of depression should therefore be made more cautiously when these conditions exist.

Children's Depression Rating Scale (CDRS)

The CDRS is another recently developed checklist that has been evaluated empirically (Poznanski, Cook, & Carroll, 1979; Poznanski, Cook, Carroll, & Corzo, 1983; Poznanski, Grossman, Buchsbaum, Banegas, Freeman, & Gibbons, 1984). This instrument is patterned after the Hamilton Depression Rating scale for adults (Hamilton, 1960). The Hamilton is the most widely used instrument in the literature for evaluating depressive symptoms. Sixteen items constitute the scale, each of which is scored by selecting among several symptoms. The child is interviewed by a trained clinician. The measure is used to evaluate children, ages 5 to 15, via three subscales addressing depressed mood and behavior, verbal expression, and fantasy. Each item is rated on a 10-point scale for severity. There is good reliability on the measure and reasonably good external validity in that it correlates with other measures of depression.

Children's Depression Adjective Checklist (C-DACL)

The C-DACL (Sokoloff & Lubin, 1983) is an adaptation of the adult Depression Adjective Checklist (Lubin et al., 1967). Some data is available on this scale. It was developed primarily to be used with adolescents, and the items were designed specifically to be relevant with this group. The authors of the C-DACL manual recommend an eighth-grade reading level for this self-report measure.

The C-DACL consists of two equivalent forms of 34 items. Twenty-two items reflect depressive mood and 12 are free of such connotations. The adolescent completing the instrument is asked to state how he or she presently feels. Sokoloff and Lubin (1983) tested 50 children, 13-19 years of age.

Some evaluations of psychometric properties have been made. Internal consistency of the scale was high as were split-half reliabilities. Also, adolescent females have been tested for the construct validity of the measure. It was correlated against the Beck Depression Inventory, the adult version of the CDI. Correlations were high relative to this anchor measure, suggesting that the C-DACL is indeed measuring depression. More recently, 50 adolescent boys were tested for concurrent validity. Correlations between the C-DACL and the Self-Rating Scale of Depressed Mood were made. The boys scored significantly lower on depression than the girls, but a strong relationship between the measures emerged (Eddy & Lubin, in press).

EVALUATIONS FROM SIGNIFICANT OTHERS

The measures reviewed to this point have emphasized direct querying of the child and/or an important adult. As noted through these two chapters on asessment, multidimensional assessment of childhood depression is preferred. The Peer Nomination Inventory for Depression (PNID) is an instrument with which the reader should be familiar because it provides a different type or dimension of information when compared to other scales reviewed so far (Lefkowitz & Tesiny, 1980). This instrument has been designed so that peers may evaluate a given child, and from that standpoint, is similar to various measures of popularity and socialization or social skills that have been used for many years (Matson & Ollendick, 1988). A problem with this approach is that for inpatient and outpatient admissions it is often difficult to gain access to the school for such an extensive evaluation, and informed consent is needed from all the children in the class. This task is not particularly easy for those clinicians who have tried. Thus, the measure may at least in some cases prove unwieldy. A use for the instrument may therefore be the preliminary screening of a class of children for those persons who may require additional assessment, a topic touched upon later in the chapter. At least for social skills, and probably for depression as well, this method tends to be a highly accurate one and, therefore, may be well worth the extra trouble required in obtaining peer data.

Peer Nomination Inventory for Depression (PNID)

The PNID (Lefkowitz & Tessiny, 1980) is administered by asking each child to nominate a peer in response to 20 depression items. A child's score consists of the total number of nominations received. As one would expect with this method, internal consistency and test-retest reliability have been very high. The PNID has been validated against several other instruments as a means of establishing its efficacy in depression measurement. It has proven to be positively related to the CDI and an adapted version of the Zung.

Short Children's Depression Inventory (SCDI)

The SCDI is a modified version of the Beck Index of Depression (Carlson & Cantwell, 1979, 1980). This scale has been used with children 7 to 17 years of age referred for inpatient and outpatient treatment. The

SCDI, as the name implies, consists of only 13 items.Each item is scored on a 4-point scale. The values for these points are; *not a problem, mild problem, always a problem,* and *severe problem*. The items encompass mood, self-esteem, hopelessness, anhedonia, and guilt. This instrument has proven useful as a means of differentially diagnosing depressed persons as well as for identifying specific symptoms extending across diagnostic groups (Kazdin, 1981).

Depression Self-Rating Scale (DSRS)

Another measure of childhood depression is the Depression Self-Rating Scale (DSRS) (Birleson, 1981; Asarnow & Carlson, 1985). Asarnow and Carlson point out that the DSRS is a scale that the clinician may consider due to limitations that they feel characterize the CDI. They point out that the CDI requires the child to select one sentence from a series of three sentences that must be considered simultaneously. They conclude that this assessment format may tax the attention span of many children (perhaps comprehension abilities as well). The shorter length and easy-to-follow format of the DSRS may be beneficial in this regard. For example, it might allow for the interviewing of younger children and those with hyperactivity, learning disabilities, and/or mental retardation.

In a study by Asarnow and Carlson (1985), 82 children ranging in age from 6 to 13 who were inpatients in the Department of Psychiatry at UCLA Medical School were tested. Sixteen children from this sample were diagnosed as depressed. This group and nondepressed children were compared on the DSRS. The authors were able to differentiate between depressed and nondepressed children. Items that showed statistically significant differences were: *I feel like crying, I feel like running away, I get stomachaches, I have horrible dreams, I feel very lonely,* and *I feel so sad I can hardly stand it*. Given the very high discriminative power of these particular items, a short form of the scale might be considered for diagnostic purposes. However,it should be pointed out that additional items, although they may not greatly enhance the reliability of diagnoses, may be of considerable value in identifying additional problem areas for psychological therapies or for evaluating treatment outcome using psychological or pharamacological interventions. Some additional findings also resulted from this study. DSRS cutoff scores were generated that produced overall rates of correct classifications ranging from 66% to 77% with very few false positives (nondepressed children classified as depressed) and the DSRS was correlated with the CDI producing very high scores. This checklist has value, and based on these data the reader may wish to consider its use.

SUMMARY

As the reader can readily see from this review there is an impressive number of childhood measures of depression within the general ruberic of checklists. Most of them seem to have considerable value and readability. However, only the CDI and RADS currently have adequate normative data. At this point the field would best be served by extensive testing of existing scales rather than the development of even more measures of childhood and adolescent depression. However, it is likely that additional instruments will proliferate.

The clinician should be comforted by the fact that the available instrumentation for measuring childhood depression far exceeds the measures available for other forms of childhood psychopathology. This is fortunate in that it shows a general interest among researchers to learn more about the topic and how best to evaluate this emotional disorder in children. Thus, what has happened with respect to scale development in terms of reliability and validity is considerable when compared to other childhood and most adult problems.

MEASURES RELATED TO DEPRESSION

Measures related to depression can be grouped into two general categories; instruments that measure a dimension of depression and general measures of psychopathology having a subset of items that characterize the disorder. Depression is a cluster of symptoms that appear together in various ways. Additional dimensions may exist for various types of depression. A review of what we currently know about these related dimensions of depression follows.

Measures of the Dimensions of Depression

Hopelessness about the future is considered a central feature of depression (Beck, 1976) and has been shown to correlate with depression in adults (Wetzel, Margulies, Davis, & Karam, 1980). Given these findings, a measure of hopelessness has also been recently developed for children (Kazdin, French, Unis, Esveldt-Dawson, & Sherick, 1983). It has been found that this measure correlates highly with suicide attempts and has internal consistency and test-retest reliability over a six-week period (Kazdin, Rodgers, & Colbus, 1986). A list of the interitem correlations of the items in the scale are depicted in Table 3-2.

Currently, professionals do not understand all of the dimensions of depression. Understanding this information is important, however, con-

Table 3–2. The Hopelessness Scale for Children: Items and item-total score correlations

	Item	Item total
1.	I want to grow up because I think things will be better (F).	0.36**
2.	I might as well give up because I can't make things better for myself (F).	0.45**
3.	When things are going badly, I know they won't be bad all of the time (F).	0.43**
4.	I can imagine what my life will be when I'm grown up (F).	0.10*
5.	I have enough time to finish the things I really want to do (F).	0.44**
6.	Someday, I will be good at doing the things I really care about (F).	0.37**
7.	I will get more of the good things in life than most other kids (F).	0.22**
8.	I don't have good luck, and there's no reason to think I will when I grow up (T).	0.51**
9.	All I can see ahead of me are bad things, not good things (T).	0.58**
10.	I don't think I will get what I really want (T).	0.48**
11.	When I grow up, I think I will be happier than I am now (F).	0.40**
12.	Things just won't work out the way I want them to (T).	0.48**
13.	I never get what I want, so it's dumb to want anything (T).	0.50**
14.	I don't think I will have any real fun when I grow up (T).	0.54**
15.	Tomorrow seems unclear and confusing to me (T).	0.41**
16	I will have more good times than bad times (F).	0.47**
17.	There's no use in really trying to get something I want because I probably won't get it (T).	0.56**

Note: An item is scored as reflecting hopelessness if the patient's answer, true (T) or false (F), agrees with that noted at the end of each item.
*$p < .05$. **$p < .001$

sidering the frequency of the disorder and the fact that many children will suffer from this dysfunction while others may suffer relapses and even make suicide attempts (Asarnow & Carlson, 1985; Kaslow & Rehm, 1983; Kovacs, Feinberg, Crouse-Novak, Paulauskas, & Finkelstein, 1984). Various parameters of depression may be important in both diagnosis and treatment of the condition. Additionally, thereoretical bases of childhood depression, only recently explored, have related helplessness and self-esteem to childhood depression (Kaslow, Rehm, & Siegal, 1984; Lefkouitz & Tesiny, 1980). It is not surprising, then, that other studies have been conducted using scales aimed at evaluating parameters of depression without directly testing the syndrome using DSM III-R criteria.

Kazdin et al. (1983) in their efforts to relate hopelessness to depression used the Coopersmith Self-Esteem Inventory. This scale is a 58-item instrument that measures self-concept and personal worth within the general construct of hopelessness. There are 58 items the child can rate as *like myself* or *not like myself*. Kazdin et al. found high correlations with the Coopersmith and the hopelessness measure. Thus, both of these instruments would seem to be important parameters of childhood depression. Yet to be determined are the specific parameters best used for evaluating childhood depression. However, age, chronicity, and type of childhood depression might prove to be some of the dimensions. More recently Asarnow, Carlson, and Guthrie (1987) have shown a strong relationship between ratings of depression, coping strategies, and family environment. It would seem prudent, then, that for children who are initially identified as depressed on the CDI, other childhood depression measures or a global instrument of childhood psychopathology would also be used. Instruments to assess helplessness, for example, should be considered. Following this procedure might allow clinicians to evaluate other dimensions or aspects of the disorder. Hopefully, more information will appear on this topic in the near future.

Social skills is another factor closely related to depression. Helsel and Matson (1984) found a strong relationship between scores on the Matson Evaluation of Social Skills with Youngsters (MESSY) and depression using the CDI. Social skills training has been an important part of treatment for this problem and is discussed in Chapter 5. The Lewinsohn (1975) and Hersen and associates (e.g., Hersen, Eisler, & Miller, 1974) research with adults most closely confirms this approach with children.

A variety of discrete social interpersonal responses may be identified using the MESSY or other measures of social skills. For example, failure to initiate interaction, make eye contact, or engage in other overt and positive behaviors may lead to or exacerbate depression. Identifying and treating these problems, as is the case with low self-esteem potentially identified with the Hopelessness Scale, are likely to be of considerable value in successfully overcoming childhood depression. The MESSY has been the most heavily researched of the social skills measures. The initial sample studied included 744 children between 4 and 18 years of age. They were tested in the Midwest in both private and public schools. Two samples were drawn from the original list, with 422 children being randomly assigned to a self-report group and 322 children rated by their teacher. The scale began with 92 items selected from general scales of psychopathology, behaviors targeted in social skills studies and clinical observations and discussions with professionals. Interrater reliability of the target behaviors was computed, and items with poor reliability were dropped to bring the final total of items to 62 for the self-report version and 64 for the teacher report (see Tables 3-1 and 3-2).

The scale has also been factor analyzed and this information may prove beneficial for the clinician developing a treatment plan for depressed children and youth (see Table 3-3). This is particularly the case if the Lewinsohn model of depression is adopted.

A second social skills measure to consider is the TROSS-C (Clark, Gresham, & Elliott, 1985). These test developers selected items from other rating scales, target behaviors that had been employed in empir-

Table 3–3.

Example 1	Instruments Used in Example Assessment (12 year old girl – outpatient). 1. Obtain background information via informal interview (child and parent). 2. Administer Child Behavior Checklist (child and parent). 3. Administer MESSY. 4. Administer Kiddie-SADS (child and parent). 5. Administer CDI (child and parent). 6. Ask specific questions that will help develop treatment. 7. Consult DSM-III-R. 8. Formulate Diagnosis and Treatment Plan.

ically based studies of social skills and social behaviors which have been shown to predict peer acceptance and/or popularity. There are 52 items on the TROSS-C to be completed by the teacher. Some items are (a) completes classroom assignments within required time, (b) uses free time in an acceptable manner, (c) interacts with peers, (d) invites peers to play, and (e) praises peers. The primary difference between the MESSY and the TROSS-C is that the latter focuses more specifically on school behavior.

In an initial study, children with normal IQs were evaluated and concurrent validity was established (Clark et al., 1985). In a later study developmentally disabled children and normal children were studied (Gresham, Elliott, & Black, 1986). There were 250 children in the sample who had been mainstreamed and who evinced problem behaviors, learning disabilities, or mild mental retardation, and also those with no handicap. Ratings by special education teachers (who evaluated the students in their classes), when factor analyzed, replicated the results found in the first study using nonhandicapped children only. The general conclusion that can be drawn from this study is that this measure is a reliable and valid means of identifying and evaluating gains in social skills. These behaviors could be ancillary to childhood depression, and information of this sort should prove valuable in the development of an overall treatment plan for these children. More on these issues are noted in the treatment chapter to follow.

Another group of behavioral assessment methods is specific to the identification of reinforcement. This approach is viewed as important with the depressed individual, since loss of reinforcement is viewed as a major factor in the increase of depressive behavior. Because of the widespread belief that reinforcement does have a major role to play in the bipolar disorder, several checklists have been developed to better study this phenomenon. A brief review of several of these instruments is provided.

The Pleasant Events Schedule (PES) lists up to 320 positive events, for example, eating good foods. The patient is asked to indicate the frequency with which each event occurred within the past 30 days on a three-point scale: 1 – not happened, 2 – a few (1-6) times, and 3 – open (7 or more times). Next, the person goes through the list a second time, indicating how pleasant and enjoyable each event was, again in a three-point format (1 – not pleasant, 2 – somewhat pleasant, and 3 – very pleasant). Scores that may be derived are: (1) activity level, which is the sum of the frequency rating; (2) reinforcement potential, the sum of the pleasantness ratings; and (3) obtained reinforcement, the sum of the product of the frequency and pleasantness ratings for each item. Not only does this scale evaluate a particular dimension of depression, but it may also be used as a means of evaluating treatment outcome. Most checklists are not sufficiently sensitive to treatment effects. This, then, is a major advantage of the PES.

Finally, one part of PES assessment is self-monitoring, which is also a component of many treatment plans. Thus, the assessment becomes not only an evaluation, but possibly part of the treatment plan. On the negative side, the measure is not normed on children. Also, depressed people tend to underestimate the frequency of past pleasant events and successful experiences (Kuiper, 1978). Once again, this information has been gathered with adults but is also likely to be the case with children.

The Reinforcement Survey Schedule is another instrument adopted for adults that suggests possible utility with children (Cautela & Kastenbaum, 1967). There are four main sections. In sections one through three, the respondent is asked to rate items on the five-point scale representing the degree of joy or pleasure derived by the patient. The first part refers to food preferences. Section two consists of 54 items that could be presented only through facsimile or imagination, including activities such as watching sports (nine types listed), playing sports, watching TV, and sleeping. Section three presents vignettes of potentially positive situations and the patient's response. On the final part of the exam the patient is asked to list things they do or think about more than 5, 10, 15, or 20 times a day. The Premack principle (high-rate behaviors can be used to reinforce low-rate behaviors) can be utilized as a means of improving the person's depressed behavior.

Another of these measures developed for use with children is referred to as the Mediator-Reinforcer Incomplete Blank (MRB) (Tharp & Wetzel, 1960). The scale consists of 34 items using an incomplete sentence format. In their original study, Tharp and Wetzel read items from the MRB aloud to the child. Patients were asked to describe reinforcers clearly and to specify referent behaviors when negative and positive statements were made about them. Thus, a person who says that the best reward (s)he could get would be love, would be asked what they would like people to do to show their love. The number of times a patient mentions a particular reinforcer or potential mediator and the tone of voice used are employed by the interviewer in assessing the relative strength and importance to patients regarding various reinforcers. Finally, all the stated reinforcers are ranked from most to least pleasant. Alternately, the authors suggest that the reinforcers may be rated from 1 to 9 as follows: (9) highly reinforcing, rarely fails to be effective; (7–8) quite reinforcing, will work hard for it (or to avoid it); (5–6) reinforces fairly well, moderate effectiveness; (4–3) weak reinforcer, only works sometimes; (1–2) has reinforcing property of a very low or indeterminate power.

These measures point to several possible methods of identifying reinforcers for psychologically based treatments. In addition to pinpointing specific deficit areas, these scales or homemade measures should prove quite useful in evaluating treatment outcome. The reinforcer methods are not designed to be a means of diagnosing any particular disorder. Recall the previous discussion of measures used for either diagnosis or measuring treatment effects.

General Measures of Psychopathology

General measures of psychopathology in children are often used as screening instruments. In this regard, various aspects of depression and their relationship to other forms of psychopathology may be identified early on in the assessment process. Therefore, the reader should have some familiarity with these scales. Only measures with well-established normative data, reliability, and validity are reviewed here. The reader should be aware that a number of instruments with psychometric properties that have been less well established are available. Also, there are a substantial number of these scales. Thus, the most popular general measures and those with empirical data relating them to general depression in children will be reviewed.

Child Behavior Checklist (CBC). Perhaps the best measure of general childhood psychopathology is the CBC (Achenbach, 1978a; Achenbach & Edelbrock, 1979). The greatest strength of this factor-analyzed scale compared to other measures of childhood psychopathology is the fact that close approximations of DSM-III diagnoses are possible. The factors of the CBC include depressed, schizoid, uncommunicative, obsessive-compulsive, somatic complaints, social withdrawal, hyperactive, aggressive, and delinquent. Thus, while the Behavior Problem Checklist (Quay & Peterson, 1967) has been more extensively researched, it has not been in common use in clinical practice due to its failure to establish factors that relate to commonly accepted diagnostic categories. It has been used extensively in research in the United States and Canada. This fact is important because other professionals are likely to be familiar with the measure.

The Child Behavior Checklist was factor analyzed based on parent ratings of 2,300 clinic-referred children and normed on 1,300 nonreferred children. More recent versions, with direct observations and self-report, have been developed. There are 118 items that take approximately 20–30 minutes to complete. Based on the parent's reading level, the clinician may wish to work closely with the parent, teacher, or child to ensure comprehensive assessment. (The reader is referred to a discussion of this issue in Chapter 2.) The various dimensions of the scale and its popularity make it a very useful childhood measure.

Personality Inventory for Children (PIC). Another measure deserving of mention because it has been used specifically with depressed children, the PIC, which was developed for completion by the child's parents (Wirt, Lachar, Klinedurst, & Seat, 1977). It consists of 600 true/false items that cover 16 clinical scales and 17 supplmental scales. The depression scale has 46 items; the child's mother but not his or her father reports scores of depression. Significant effects for depressed children were evident. These findings replicate a previous study (Leon, Kendall, & Garber, 1980). The data suggest that the PIC would be a second instrument of general psychopathology that may be employed to narrow the childhood disorder to depression. It has not had the widespread use of the CBC however. The PIC is a long measure in terms of time for completion, and this may make its use less practical or relevant in some clinical settings.

ASSESSMENT MODEL

This chapter and the previous one have presented a review of particular types of assessments. There are certain procedures the clinician may wish to consider in overall evaluation; following are some suggestions as to the manner in which to proceed. If possible, assessment should include direct observation, preferably in a standardized activity, interviewing the client, reviewing DSM-III-R criteria, and employing at least one general psychopathology checklist. Other measures would be at least two checklists of depression with self- and other report information and a measure of ancillary problems such as self-esteem.

The assessment process should proceed from general to more specialized. First, the child and parent should be interviewed briefly and the mother should be asked to fill out a general psychopathology scale. The

Child Behavior Checklist is particularly useful given that subfactors related to DSM-III-R, such as depression, emerge. The amount of time required to complete the scale, how clear-cut the symptoms appear, and how immediately symptoms must be attended to will determine whether the assessment battery should be completed at this point, after a brief break, or at another time. The second segment of the battery would include the administration of the specialized instruments. A diagnosis could be confirmed in this manner and efforts could be initiated to select treatment outcome measures. This evaluation would be concluded by determining a few specific target behaviors and one of two specific depression scales to evaluate treatment outcome. Also, the clinician may wish to briefly test the child on his ability to self-monitor and evaluate and to determine how conscientious the mother is in ensuring that the child carries out assignments. This latter information is likely to prove very helpful in selecting the most viable type of treatment for a given client.

Most children will be referred by parents or concerned professionals, particularly teachers. However, Reynolds (1986) also suggests using checklists as a general screening for young children. The idea is to emphasize prevention via early identification. The stages of assessment he suggests to accomplish this goal are: (1) classroom screening with self-report depression measures; (2) retesting of children who met criteria for depression during step one; and (3) conducting individual clinical interviews with children who manifest clinical levels of depression in the first two stages.

Given the large number of available measures, different measures may be useful based on age and other client characteristics. Table 3-4 and 3-5 present some examples of how these measures might be used. It should be kept in mind, however, that these are meant only as a guideline.

The clinician will need to determine whether the first model described

Table 3–4

Example 2	(8 year old boy – inpatient)*
	1. Obtain background information via informal interview (child and parent).
	2. Administer Child Behavior Checklist (child and parent).
	3. Administer MESSY (child and parent).
	4. Administer CDI (child and parent).
	5. Administer SCDI.
	6. Administer DSRS.
	7. Administer direct observation measure.
	8. Consult DSM-III-R.
	9. Formulate Diagnosis and Treatment Plan.

*Note that age and whether the child is an inpatient or outpatient will to some degree dictate the assessment instruments used. As a general rule the Kiddie-SADS should be used only for older children with good verbal comprehension and good attention span. Direct observation is particularly good for younger children but may be practical in most instances only with inpatient children.

Table 3–5. Checklists for measuring depression

General Psychopathology
Child Behavior Checklist (Achenbach and Edelbrock, 1979)
Personality Inventory for Children (Wirt, Lachar, Klinedurst, and Seat, 1977)
Child Depression
Child Depression Inventory (Kovacs and Beck, 1977)
Reynolds Adolescent Depression Scale (Reynolds, 1987)
Children's Depression Scale (Tisher and Lang, 1983)
Children's Depression Rating Scale (Poznanski, et al., 1979)
Children's Depression Adjective Checklist (Lubin and Zuckerman, 1967)
Peer Nomination Inventory for Children (Lefkowitz and Tesiny, 1980)
Short Children's Depression Inventory (Cantwell, 1983)
Depression Self-Rating Scale (Birleson, 1981)
Related Measures
Coopersmith Self-Esteem Inventory (Kazdin, French, Unis, Eveldt-Dawson, & Sherick, 1983)
Matson Evaluation of Social Skills with Youngsters (Matson, Helsel, 1983)

Note. An effort had been made to obtain permission from the various publishers to reprint their scales. However, the general policy for most publishers is not to do so. Should you wish to obtain the measures please consult a reference for the senior author of each measure. They will be able to provide pertinent information for reviewing and purchasing the various testing materials recommended in this book.

above alone is sufficient or whether it should be combined with the Reynold's approach. It should be noted that most parents have some general concept of depression. Therefore, another possibility may be to give talks to parent and teacher groups about spotting childhood depression. Such a method would fall somewhere between model one and the combination of the two models described above. Regardless of the approach selected, however, it is useful to have an overall system for evaluation.

SUMMARY

This chapter presented a review of various checklists for evaluating childhood depression. Given the number of scales available, a table to briefly summarize them is presented for the convenience of the reader in Table 3-5. While this list may not be all-inclusive, the major scales have been covered, particularly with respect to those having good empirical support. There are an impressive number of instruments relative to the broad field of childhood psychopathology. Many of these instruments still require considerable development before they can be used to provide consistent, valid, and reliable diagnostic information. Additionally, most of the scales correlate highly, are parent or child report, and could be categorized as duplicates of each other.

The recommended approach would be to use the CBC as a general measure of child psychopathology. Given a positive outcome on depression, the CDI and/or RADS, preferably with both self- and other report (parent, direct-care staff, or teacher) could be combined with a structured interview such as the Kiddie-SADS and any other general questioning that the therapist would like to conduct. One or more other measures might be considered with respect to the particular problem presented by a given client. Data from these various sources could then be summed to make a diagnosis. The information obtained in this fashion could be employed for placement, identification of specific symptoms for treatment, and type of treatment. Evaluating treatment outcome could be performed by using one or two specific measures in the format described in Chapter 2.

Obviously, the range of procedures selected for evaluating treatment outcome is of great importance. It should be emphasized that the development of a systematic battery of measures is of considerable utility and should be a primary consideration for the clinician who is attempting to evaluate children likely to evince depressive symptomatology. The next step is treating the disorder, the topic of our next section.

Chapter 4

Treatment: Developing a Treatment Plan and Cognitive Therapy

Effective treatment of depression in young persons is, of course, an extremely important issue to mental health workers. In this chapter the more popular psychological procedures for the treatment of depression in children and adolescents are discussed. The first of these two approaches is a loosely defined group of treatments often referred to as cognitive behavior therapy. These methods by and large follow the concept of learning theory/theories. There is some overlap of the cognitive methods with social learning theory in that covert modeling and other imaging and mental processing methods constitute a major thrust of these programs. Additionally, however, self-control procedures are also a major component of this approach. Among this latter group of methods are self-monitoring and covert reinforcement. These and other related techniques will be covered shortly.

The second model to be discussed is family therapy. In this instance, more traditional behavioral methods are applied within the family unit. The notion that the child's problems are often partially or perhaps solely due to family dysfunction is discussed. And from this standpoint the goal of treatment varies somewhat from client-directed procedures, which constitute the bulk of other available treatments. A stronger argument for this approach can be built with recent research showing the effect of parental mood, both negative and positive, on child behavior. For example, considerable research relating depression in the mother to childhood problems of similar forms has been reported.

Some of the best developments in this regard follow. First, however, a brief example of interview material and the general structure that can be followed in delivering these types of therapies is provided.

DEVELOPING A TREATMENT PLAN

Cognitive behavior therapy, like behavior therapy approaches, tends to be structured and of short duration. These characteristics of treatment are particularly important for children and adolescents and may be viewed as assets. The major focus of therapy is to work with clients in an effort to change attitudes toward the world in which they interact. If this program is used, the child should be seen 3–5 times per week in a school by a psychologist and 2–3 times if being seen on an outpatient basis. Two times per week is the typical regimen for adults. However, children should generally be seen for shorter time intervals (e.g., 30 minutes rather than the customary 50–60 minutes for adults). Often we will see the child alone and then see the child with one or both parents for the remainder of the session. In this way an effort is made to involve the parents in homework activities and in reporting back on life events between treatment sessions. Also, this mix allows for continued and ongoing informal assessment of the child's behavior alone, within the dynamics of the family situation and over time. It is suggested by some proponents of cognitive and other versions of behavior therapy that the number of sessions may be decreased as therapy progresses. It is recommended that the treatment of children should generally follow this approach–sessions can be decreased to once a week, once every two weeks, and then once a month before treatment is terminated. This approach allows for gradually fading the therapist from the treatment environment while allowing for follow-up of treatment and for booster training sessions.

The content of the first two sessions should focus on defining and assessing the problem and helping to teach the client and his family what therapy is about. Session one might start with a description of the clinic, the fee schedule, and a description of the problem that brought them to the psychologist/social worker/child psychiatrist/psychiatric nurse or other professional who will be providing treatment. It is important to help the child and parents quantify the problem. The child may or may not be included in this initial session. Preference, from this author's perspective is to see the parents alone to gain a better notion of the most appropriate method for working with the child. Also, by seeing the parents alone, the potential embarrassment the child may feel in being talked about while present may be avoided. An exception would be particularly likely with a highly verbal older child or adolescent who could participate more fully in the discussion.

Defining the problem should consist of operationalizing observable behavior. For example, initial remarks by the client or his or her family might include whether the client is suicidal. As in several cases seen by this author, upon further questioning it becomes clear that suicide attempts are sometimes not that at all. Rather, in some cases they may consist of the child cutting his or her hair or throwing a temper tantrum consisting of yelling and throwing his or her self on the floor. In these instances the problem is often one of poor management and/or communication between parent(s) and the child and may or may not have depression as a secondary problem to adjustment in the home or school environment. If more typical signs of depression, such as withdrawal, lack of interest in activities, or other classic signs are evident, then an assessment using the types of procedures described in previous chapters would be in order and would be scheduled for the second meeting.

The remainder of the first session would focus on a developmental history and review of environmental events leading up to the effort of seeing a therapist. An example of the questions and answers likely to occur in a hypothetical case are presented in the following dialogue. These questions would, of course, be paired with the various assessment methods reviewed in the last two chapters.

Therapist: Typically, it is valuable to determine when your child was able to perform various tasks such as sitting up and crawling. Therefore, I need to ask you some questions and would appreciate whatever information you can remember. If it is difficult to remember a specific point, that is okay. It is common not to remember all the various developmental milestones of your child. Please just say I can't remember. *(A problem often encountered is that the parent makes up a response to the questions if they don't know it. This tactic by the parent may present a problem to the examiner. If milestones are grossly inaccurate, this can typically be identified [e.g., my child began to walk at 5 months and talk in complete sentences at 7 months]).* Let's start with your pregnancy. Was there anything unusual that happened?

Client: Not that I can think of.

Therapist: How about smoking, heavy drinking, or other lifestyle activities that could potentially be problematic.

Client: No, I didn't do anything of that sort.

Therapist: When did your child sit up, begin to crawl and walk?

Client: Everything was about normal I think. He started to sit up at 3 months, crawled at 6 months and walked at 11 months.

Therapist: Did anything traumatic or unusual psychologically happen prior to school?

Client: Everything was fine.

Therapist: How about during the first five years of school through fourth grade?

Client: Well everything was pretty much okay. He did have some trouble in his schoolwork, making C's, and D's, and he did flunk a class or two. He seemed to like school okay, though, until fifth grade when things really started to get bad.

Therapist: Could you tell me what you mean.

Client: Well his grades went way down, and he started to complain about going to school. In the mornings he would say he was sick. Also, he said kids at school were making fun of him. And, he said it wasn't worth trying at school or talking to kids because nothing worked out anyway.

Based on these initial remarks the therapist could then lead the client into a discussion of specific behaviors and behavioral attributes that would be helpful in targeting responses for therapy. Emphasis on identifying discrete responses for treatment will fit in specifically with the treatment procedures discussed later in this chapter and the next chapter.

Oftentimes, a useful approach is to have the mother join in discussions with the child and therapist, particularly with young children. This approach is considered useful since homework is often an important part of treatment and, particularly for those children who are not yet in high school, there may be difficulty carrying through on tasks without assistance. Some of these components include structured activity schedules (perhaps as frequently as once per hour), graded task assignments such as getting out of bed, getting dressed, eating specific types and amounts of food, and grooming. Other skills include self-monitoring of tasks, covert behavioral rehearsal (the person thinks about, then goes over this information in his or her own mind regarding how best to carry out specific behaviors). Searching for alternative solutions to the problems is another approach often used in cognitive therapy. With the client, a review is made of various options that the person might substitute for ineffective responses that are displayed. Once an effective treatment is established, sessions might be gradually decreased in frequency (once every two weeks versus once or twice a week). Variations of these components in the order presented here are routinely followed. Following this general organization of evaluation and treatment, the particular strategies will vary. Some of these variations follow.

COGNITIVE BEHAVIOR THERAPY

As previously noted, cognitive-behavior therapy is a term that has come to refer to a diverse group of treatment approaches (Rehm & Kornblith, 1979). A variety of approaches falls under this category with the following characteristics being among those differentiating the approach: directive, structured, goal-directed, time-limited, learning-theory based, emphasis on covert along with overt behaviors, employing homework, practice of skills specified by the therapist, emphasis on increasing the client's adaptive problem-solving skills by teaching specific strategies, working together with the client, and the emphasis on cognitions as defined as behavioral events important in the therapy process

(Kovacs, 1981). Thinking and evaluation, *unlike* the performance of discrete behaviors stressed in the operant and social learning strategies discussed in the next chapter, are viewed as *the* key to developing and understanding the problem of depression. Cognitions are viewed as processes that mediate stimuli and as responses, and these cognitions should be the primary focus for modification.

Cognitive behavior therapy is a well-accepted method of treatment, particularly with adult patients. Perhaps the best known and most popular of these methods is the program of Beck and associates (Beck, Rush, Shaw, & Emery, 1979). This approach stresses the etiological importance of cognitive variables, with various behaviors within the social learning domain playing a lesser role (e.g., Lewinsohn, 1975). The central aspect of the approach of Beck et al. is the three-part cognitive model. The approach relies on attributes or views of oneself based on life events. One aspect of this approach, negative view of self, centers around the concept of oneself as inadequate, worthless, and generally deficient. The second component consists of the individual's perceptions of his interactions with the environment. And, in almost all cases, even the most positive events are somehow misconstrued in a negative manner by the depressed individual. For example, if a person compliments the depressed individual for a job well done, the afflicted person is likely to say that the individual making the compliment only made the remark because he felt sorry for the depressed individual or wanted something from him. Third, the depressed individual's view of the future is, in general, a very negative one. Perceptions of impending doom, hopelessness, likelihood for failure, and related unpleasant perceptions lead the person to an unhappy, unfulfilled life. The specifics may differ with related theories of depression; however, one common theme holds true. The person generally leads a negative lifestyle where his or her perceptions and attitudes almost always minimize positives and accentuate negatives. This formulation is significant because it constitutes those aspects viewed to be the most important factors requiring attention in treatment.

These misperceptions are also called misattributions. The individual interprets behavior incorrectly, and these perceptions must be changed. As with other psychological therapies, the more common unipolar depressive is the primary target for treatment. Verbal and imagining skills, along with the willingness and motivation to follow through with homework, are important if treatement is to prove successful.

Treatment Components

There are several common treatment components employed in cognitive behavioral therapy and, to a lesser extent, some other behaviorally oriented treatments. Among these methods are self-monitoring, activity scheduling, cognitive restructuring, attribution retraining, self-evaluation, and self-reinforcement. Since these concepts are used throughout this chapter, each of them is briefly described.

Self-Monitoring. This procedure involves observing one's own behavior whether internal or external. Self-recording of responses using either an unstructured form or checking a list of predetermined target responses may also be viewed as part of this technique. Self-monitoring has been effectively used with children and adolescents (Reynolds & Coats, in press; Stark, Reynolds, & Kaslow, in press). Several specific procedures have been described in the literature and are briefly reviewed later in this chapter.

Because children often have trouble thinking of pleasant events, Reynolds and Stark (1985) developed a short questionnaire as an aid. Current and age-appropriate activities are provided for the child's inspection and endorsement. This approach may also prove of value in identifying children who do not seem to derive pleasure from typical childhood activities and who may be depressed. The authors also stress that it may serve as a diary of activities and pleasant thoughts. Such an approach is highly recommended since it adds further systematization and structure to treatment.

Activity Schedules. This method involves the systematic planning of the youngster's daily schedule. Together, the therapist and child plan daily goals. The aim is to decrease negative and increase positive thoughts and activities. Particular attention is put on activities that enhance mood, affect, and self-esteem.

Cognitive Restructuring. The basics of this technique can be traced to Albert Ellis. The term refers to realignment of thinking to change the depressed child's or adolescent's maladaptive style of processing information (Rimm & Masters, 1979). Depressed people often view themselves negatively and the world around them as hostile. Beck (1967) identifies six basic errors in processing information including: (1) arbitrary inferences; (2) selective abstraction; (3) overgeneralization; (4) magnification and minimization; (5) personalization; and (6) absolute, dichotomous thinking. While the specific categories may differ, most cognitive therapies include one or more of these schema. Inaccurate thinking and processing factors are involved largely in this component of the cognitive behavioral program.

Attribution Retraining. Attributions refer to the cognitive style in which the person interprets external events. The focus of this process, therapeutically speaking, especially with children and adolescents, is the focus on teaching children about attribution and how it can be used adaptively. Hypothetical situations are used, after which the child is asked to give his interpretation of the event. Based on the child's feedback, a determination can be made of the appropriateness of this attribution in promoting healthy thinking. Appropriate remediation strategies may then be followed to enhance adaptive behavior.

Self-Evaluation. Cognitive processes are compared to one's performance with an internal standard. It has been hypothesized that depression is a distortion in the self-evaluation process. This situation results in the setting of excessively stringent, unattainable standards of performance. It has been established that children can be accurately trained to evaluate this behavior (Spates & Kanfer, 1977). An effort is made to assist the youngster in discrepancies between the standard for performance and its evaluation. Procedures such as those mentioned previously and later in this chapter could be used in establishing more acceptable standards.

Self-Reinforcement. A final procedure is self-reward, contingent on the occurrence of appropriate behavior. This aspect of therapy is referred to as self-reinforcement. This technique is often used with cognitive approaches and may be viewed as a self-control method. The therapist helps the client define specific tasks which the client is to complete. The behavior, when finished correctly, can be self-reinforced in a variety of ways. These include rewarding oneself by going shopping, eating a preferred food, or by giving oneself a tangible reward. Covert social reinforcers—for instance, thinking about what a good job one has done—is another possible approach.

These procedures and variations of them are typically used with most cognitive therapies. More detail is presented later in this chapter on specific variations of cognitive behavior therapy.

Common Cognitive Therapies

More traditional cognitive or cognitive behavioral approaches are available, although to date they have not been used as frequently with children. Rational emotive therapy, developed by Ellis (1962), is certainly of note. Unfortunately, there is not sufficient empirical evidence to support the value of this method. Nonetheless, it is worth at least a brief review given its widespread popularity in clinical settings despite the lack of a solid data base.

Rational-Emotive Therapy. Rationale-emotive therapy is based on the notion that people have faulty beliefs about themselves such as, "everyone should like me." The acceptance of this notion leads the client to a poor self-view and this may lead in turn, to low self-esteem, social withdrawal, and other behaviors that make up depression. The treatment, as most readers are probably aware, consists of getting the client to re-evaluate or restructure his thinking. This approach allows the client to develop more positive attitudes and behavior. Treatment does not focus on the emotionality or emotional level of the client. Rather, the focus is on thinking problems through and on rational decision making. There are several basic assumptions that are made and these dictate how treatment is carried out. They include: (1) Man is uniquely rational and irrational, and when rational is effective, happy, and competent; (2) Psychological stress is a result of irrational and illogical thinking; (3) Illogical thinking comes from family and culture; (4) Symbolic language is the usual and best way of problem solving; (5) Emotional states are determined not by external circumstances but by the perceptions and attitudes toward these events; and (6) Negative and self-defeating thoughts and emotions must be reorganized in a more logical fashion.

The concept of irrational thoughts is the core problem and the central focus of the Ellis (1962) treatment model. He has listed 11 central irrational thoughts. They are: (1) It is esssential that one be loved or approved by virtually everyone; (2) One must be perfectly competent, adequate, and achieving to consider oneself worthwhile; (3) Some people are bad, wicked, or villainous and therefore should be blamed and punished; (4) It is a terrible catastrophe when things are not as one wants them to be; (5) Unhappiness is caused by outside circumstances and the individual has no control over it; (6) Dangerous or fearsome things are causes for great concern, and their possibility must be continually dwelt upon; (7) It is easier to avoid difficulties and self-responsibilities than to face them; (8) One should be dependent on others and must have someone stronger on whom to rely; (9) Past experiences and events are the determiners of present behavior; the influence of the past cannot be eradicated; (10) One should be quite upset over other people's problems and disturbances; and (11) There is always a right or perfect solution to every problem, and it must be found or the results will be catastrophic.

These problems are discussed and reviewed with the client, and examples are given with regard to the 11 points. Then, a new and more adaptive course is determined. These are accomplished by discussion in therapy and via homework.

Little research has been conducted to support the efficacy of this method. However, most graduate programs in behavior therapy and most volumes that discuss cognitive behavioral methods review this approach in some detail. It is likely that this trend has developed since Rational-Emotive Therapy was described far earlier than other cognitive behavioral methods, and since various components of this approach have been included in other empirically supported treatments. Some of these methods are discussed later in this chapter.

Beck Method. Beck's cognitive therapy employs a premise similar to the general cognitive behavioral methods noted above and has also been studied empirically. Treatment focuses on negative thoughts, attitudes, and other maladaptive ways in which behavior is processed. Beck's model differs from the Ellis model in that more latitude is used for the system in which the behavior is reviewed. The 11 faulty beliefs of Ellis, noted above, are not employed. Rather, a loose group of generally faulty modes of thinking is evaluated. Typical problem areas discussed with this approach include the tendency to magnify the imporatnce of personality and relevant unfavorable events and to minimize meaningful positive events or attributes. The approach follows the commonly held and empirically documented notion that the patient selectively remembers unpleasant situations or events and persistently draws conclusions through the misinterpretation of these situations or events (Beck, 1963). The notion of cognitive templates (ways of organizing, interpreting, or construing particular sets of experiences) are endorsed (Kovacs & Beck, 1979). Individual-specific internal or external cues viewed as significant in survival and/or self-esteem are at issue.

This therapy has been studied primarily with adults but may also prove viable for treating adolescents and some children. Treatment has generally been administered in brief periods (about 12 weeks) in individual sessions. The clients are given didactic explanations of the relationship among cognition, affect and behavior, and ways that concepts relate to the phenomenology of depression. Through their own life experiences, the clients are taught to observe and record their maladaptive cognitions. Clients learn to question and evaluate responses to various external events and help determine what is appropriate or inappropriate accordingly. Homework assignments in the course of daily living are used to help patients test the validity of their opinions and be able to deal more effectively with problem situations. Homework is also used to employ strategies such as daily activity schedules and counting negative thoughts. This approach and the others in this chapter differ from the operant and social learning methods in that the focus is on modifying internal versus external states and/or events. One study with 32 mild and moderately depressed 18- to 25-year-old persons treated over a four-week period found that these patients responded well to this approach (Shaw, 1977).

The effectiveness of the Beck et al. (1979) program has received considerable empirical support (Hollin, Ierubeis, Tuason, Evans, Weimer, &

Garvey, 1984; Murphy, Simons, Wetzel, & Lustman, 1984). It has been concluded by some that this approach is as effective as pharmacological intervention and may aid in preventing depressive relapses (Kovacs, Rush, Beck, & Hollin, 1981).

A treatment program developed and tested specifically for children is described by Reynolds and Coats (1986). From an initial pool of 800 students from a midwestern high school, they picked 30 persons, 11 male and 19 female, who met criteria for depression. The cognitive behavior therapy program consisted of training in self-control skills such as self-monitoring, self-evaluation and self-reinforcement. Other basic training techniques in the five-week program included a behavior change plan employing the components described above. Sessions consisted of a presentation and a discussion of self-control principles relevant to the hypothesized deficits found in depression, with the remaining time devoted to the assignment of homework exercises and a review of the preceding session's assignment.

Session one of the program began with a description of cognitive behavior therapy presented in common language, devoid of most technical terms. Self-monitoring was then reviewed, stressing the importance of accurate self-observation to influence mood. A discussion of how depressed persons tend to overattend to unpleasant mood was emphasized. Next, clients were given daily logs for monitoring activities and moods. Remaining sessions began with a short summary of the rationale and format of the last assignment.

For the second treatment session, a mood-and-activity exercise followed this explanation. Clients graphed positive activities and mood ratings for each day to help demonstrate the connection between activity and mood. Various examples were rehearsed to better establish this relationship.

The third session began with the review noted above, followed by a discussion of the tendency of depressed persons to attend to immediate versus long-term effects of their behaviors and activities. These distortions of self-concept have often been found in depressed persons, and the depressed person will often focus on less pleasant immediate reinforcers as opposed to the more important delayed forms of reinforcement (Beck, 1967). To help these depressed adolescents attend more closely to the delayed positive consequences of behavior, exercises emphasizing immediate versus delayed effects were presented.

In session four, self-evaluation began as a formal aspect of the training program, based on the notion of Beck et al. that depressed persons often hold faulty beliefs about their responsibility for events. The adolescents were taught to look closely at assumptions people make in assigning credit, blame, or responsibility.

Session five emphasized methods for developing a self-change plan consisting of (a) specifying the problem, (b) collecting baseline data, (c) discovering antecedents and consequences, (d) setting goals, (e) contracting, and (f) obtaining reinforcement. Clients were requested to identify a specific problem to work on and to begin collecting baseline data while paying attention to antecedent and consequent events.

The content of session six emphasized setting realistic and obtainable goals as part of a self-change plan. Stressed was the selection of subgoals that were positive, attainable, overt, and within the control of the client's own abilities and efforts. Clients continued to collect baseline data regarding their target problems and to develop appropriate subgoals.

Session seven involved self-reinforcement. The therapist presented general principles of reinforcement and related these to problems of depression. Clients were shown how systematic errors in thinking often lead to negative interpretations that result in excessive self-punishment with small amounts of self-reward. Clients constructed a self-reward schedule for use in their self-change plan and a schedule for monitoring small behaviors leading to larger goal behaviors. Self-administration of rewards was encouraged, using schedules to determine point values for various reinforcers. They were to reward themselves, based on predetermined goals.

Session eight included a brief presentation relating both covert self-reward and self-punishment to depression. Then, the client practiced covert self-reinforcement. These procedures were to be employed along with self-reinforcement.

The final two sessions nine and ten, were aimed at determining how well clients had complied with the procedures described above, while reviewing past practices that had been trained. Extra copies of log sheets and related forms were provided. A variety of dependent variables including the RADS and other depression measures were employed. Self-esteem and anxiety assessments also showed a marked improvement over those of persons who did not receive treatment. However, another, more traditional behavioral method employing relaxation procedures was equally effective as the cognitive program. That program is reviewed later in this chapter.

Rehm Self-Control Method. Another model relying heavily on self-control methods is described by Rehm (1977). He views self-control as the process that assists the client in altering the probabilities of a particular response in the absence of immediate external reinforcers. Depression is conceptualized as deficits in one of three component areas that define the process of self-evaluation and self-reinforcement.

Self-monitoring involves the individual's making self-observations of the antecedents and consequences of his or her behavior. It consists of the self-evaluation and self-reinforcement which are the means by which self-monitoring may be achieved. One of these processes, self-evaluation, consists of the client's looking at his estimated performance relative to a subjective criteria. With self-reinforcement, it is assumed that clients can self-administer reinforcement or punishment to increase or decrease the frequency of their behavior. This assumption can be tested with many children and adolescents. Thus, in many situations, adaptations to the treatment may be required, such as closer supervision or more external verbal and manual prompts by the therapist, parent, and teacher. Rehm (1977) identifies cognitions for remediation as selective attention toward negative events, overly restrictive self-evaluations, negative attribution style, low rates of contingent positive reinforcement, and high rates of self-monitoring. The therapist attempts to teach the client how to effectively self-reinforce his or her own behavior. Clients can be treated individually or in groups following a training schedule from one session to another similar to that described by Rehm. Obviously, with any of these or other psychological approaches, the training schedules provided should be used as a guide. Whether the therapist choses to go faster or slower should be dictated by factors such as age, motivation, and prior experience of a given client.

More recently, a variant of Rehm's model has been tested with 9 children, 5 males and 4 females, averaging 11 years of age (Stark, Reynolds, & Kaslow, 1987). The treatment was modeled after Rehm's self-control training of normal adults (Rehm, Kaslow, Rabin, & Willard, 1984). The intervention program was designed to teach children more adaptive skills for self-monitoring, self-evaluating performance, attributing the cause of good and bad outcomes, and self-consequating. These concepts were taught through didactic presentations and in therapy exercises. These skills were applied via homework assignments. A cartoon character was created and utilized to make the concepts easier to understand. Each session was designed to build on previous sessions, as described earlier in this chapter. The purpose was to provide a sequence of skills for the child as a means of attaining long-term goals such as enhanced self-worth and a more positive attitude toward others and events.

Systematic Desensitization

The procedures described above constitute a core of the more popular, traditional cognitive approaches to therapy with depressed children and adolescents. It is also useful to describe the relaxation procedures briefly mentioned earlier in this chapter, because they represent yet another possible treatment option for depressed youth. This approach consists of a modification of methods and parts of methods that have been used to treat phobic and anxious behaviors for some time (Wolpe, 1982).

Anxiety also plays a major role in depression and may, at least in part, account for the use of relaxation methods with this population. Reynolds and Coats (1986) describe a successful application of this procedure with high school students ($N = 10$). Sessions began in a manner similar to the cognitive-behavioral treatment of these authors, described in detail earlier in this chapter. An introduction of the procedures was provided, followed by a review of confidentiality issues and a general introduction to the program. For example, the relationship of stress and depression was discussed. The goal of relaxation training and the relationship between stress, muscle relaxation, and depression were reviewed.

Four sessions focused on helping the clients learn to relax by tension and relaxation of various muscle groups in line with the Jacobson (1938) procedures and as incorporated in systematic desensitization (Wolpe, 1982).

Sessions six to nine were focused primarily on helping the client generalize these relaxation skills across situations likely to produce stress, tension, or anxiety for the client. Then, in session ten, the entire program was presented and the clients were encouraged to continue using their relaxation skills in future tension-producing situations. All sessions lasted 50 minutes.

The cognitive aspect of training involved having the client think about being relaxed. Traditionally, when this treatment approach is used with phobic clients, therapy also involves having the client think about anxiety- or stress-producing situations. These situations are paired with muscle relaxation as a method of producing calm behavior when such thoughts occur rather than being nervous and agitated. The notion is that anxiety, which includes muscle tension and increased central nervous system activity, cannot occur simultaneously with relaxation. This method has very limited experimental documentation with depressed groups. However, given its extreme effectiveness and experimental documentation with anxiety and with some depressed adults it is likely to be a useful procedure, particularly where anxiety is a major component of the overall list of symptoms that characterize the depression.

Behavioral Problem Solving

Another interesting method that could be paired with the relaxation of other cognitive methods is referred to as behavioral problem solving. Stark et al. (1987) successfully used this procedure, combining self-monitoring and a pleasant activities schedule for the acquisiton of problem-solving skills. Also included was the development of skills and knowledge about feelings and social behavior that served as a forum for expressing feelings in a structured approach traditionally used in psychotherapy. Also, activities were used to teach clients about their feelings and how their behavior can affect social relationships. Self-monitoring and group problem-solving were used to increase the pleasant activity level. Skills were developed via didactic presentations and practice exercises in the form of homework. Clients also received rewards, tangible and social reinforcers.

The problem-solving approach has received some attention with other problems of children. And, this limited test of the procedure with depressed children also proved to be encouraging. Therefore, this approach is also recommended, particularly with older children and youth who have the academic background and self-discipline that would be necessary to carry out this treatment.

The methods described above constitute the best delineated and empirically supported cognitive approaches. Next, an example is presented to further illustrate some components of this group of treatments.

Sample Case

The 12-year-old girl (Jane) had been referred by her mother shortly after the parents had divorced. The separation by the parents had been very hostile and the father had failed to make contact with Jane for the past six months. This information, other demographic information, and ideas about family dynamics were provided in a discussion with the mother alone. This was followed by a brief discussion with the child and mother together. A review was made of the clinic, client fees, and the sliding scale policy for such fees. The assessment and treatment process was also described. A commitment of 12 biweekly meetings were arranged to complete the assessment and to begin treatment. It was agreed that at the conclusion of this phase, progress would be reviewed and the visits would terminate or a new contract would be established. Finally, the mother was asked to complete the Child Behavior Checklist.

Between sessions, the therapist scored the CBC. A particularly high depression profile was observed relative to the other subscales. Given the child's age and above-average verbal skills both self- and mother report on several checklists was planned and executed at the second session. The measures included the CDI, RADS, and C-DACL. The Coopersmith Self-Esteem Inventory and both the self- and informant versions of the MESSY were administered. These instruments were scored between the second and third session. Jane scored uniformly in the direction of high levels of depression, low self-esteem, and inappropriate social behavior on all of these measures. The MESSY, CDI, and RADS in particular had individual items that were used for treatment.

Jane had a male therapist. This approach was taken as a means of providing appropriate modeling by an opposite-sex adult. An approach of this sort was felt to be of value based on the mother's comments about the lack of such modeling in a one-parent household and the fact that Jane evinced various disruptive behaviors as a means of acquiring attention.

The Reynolds and Coats (1986) version of the Beck cognitive training program described earlier in this chapter was employed. Specific target behaviors (six total) selected from the MESSY, CDI, and RADS were reviewed and included self-monitoring. These items and general responses (four total) covering mood were included in Jane's daily log. This procedure was reviewed with both the mother and Jane present. Jane was asked to describe these methods back to the therapist to ensure that she could carry them out correctly. The mother was to serve as supervisor of Jane's therapy activities at home. Procedures of self-evaluation, setting goals, and developing other treatment skills were followed using the 10-session training procedure plus the two initial evaluation sessions.

Session 11 ended by re-evaluating Jane on the CDI, RADS, and MESSY. These measures were unlike the other instruments administered and were found to be useful for this particular client as measures of diagnosis and treatment outcome. Session 12 included a review of these measures and the 10 specific responses included in self-monitoring with Jane and her mother. Progress had been made but problems were still evident. A second contract of 12 sessions, one per week, was established. The assessment used at the end of session 11 was again used at the end of session 25 and reviewed at session 26. Marked improvements were noted at this point. Three meetings, one per month, were then scheduled, primarily to review progress and emphasize areas of continued improvement and the acquisition of additional adaptive responses. These meetings were the final sessions required because considerable improvement was noted by the therapist, child, and mother. It was mutually agreed that no additional therapy was needed at this time.

The final 15 sessions did not involve the addition of new procedures to the treatment plan. Rather, emphasis was on reviewing unique applications of the identification of antecedents and consequences, using self-monitoring, and attempting to enhance the 10 identified skill-deficit areas. Training sessions involved social reinforcement of Jane and her mother, corrective feedback where needed, and modeling and role playing of various skills. Half-way through treatment it also became evident that the mother required independent, individual behavior therapy as well. The focus was on helping her adjust to her current living arrangement, working on various parenting skills, and providing emotional support so she would be better able to assist her child. A female therapist worked with the mother based on her view that she would feel more open about expressing concerns to a same-sex therapist.

SUMMARY

This chapter has reviewed some general concepts, principles, and specific treatment strategies that should prove helpful to the therapist working with depressed children and adolescents. The primary focus of treatment has been with adolescents. This should come as no great surprise for those acquainted with basic developmental principles. These methods are recommended primarily for children and adolescents 12 years of age and above, although with some modifications younger children may prove to be amenable to this treatment approach. More likely, younger children will respond better to the social learning and operant methods discussed in the following chapter. It should be noted that the methods in the following chapter will likely apply to the entire age range. Specific notions concerning adaptations of these treatments to differing age groups are discussed. The methods noted in this chapter, however, are of considerable note given that they have been tested and found to be effective with children and adolescents in well-controlled experimental studies. The reader may wish to employ one of the methods described above as the central focus of treatment. Then, various aspects of the other cognitive treatments mentioned could be mixed and matched to tailor the complete treatment package for a particular child.

Chapter 5

Treatment: Social Learning, Operant and Drug Treatments

This chapter reviews additional models of treatment for depression in children and adolescents. There are many similarities and some differences between these approaches and cognitive treatments. The focus is on more overt strategies. This will become evident as the reader reviews this chapter. The first approach to be discussed is social learning theory. One method that receives particular attention is Lewinsohn's (1975) social learning program. It should be noted with this treatment, along with most others mentioned in this book, that unipolar depression is the primary problem receiving treatment. Emphasized are the importance of the environment, social skillfulness of the person, and mechanisms for providing social reinforcement to the child. Other points that are of note for this treatment approach include: (1) A child/adolescent with a poor social skills repertoire, defined as low verbal activity, passivity, problems in listening and interpreting others' behavior correctly, and the lack of adequate skills in dispensing positive reinforcement to others, results in failure to elicit available reinforcers in the environment; (2) Events that are contingent on the person's behavior may not be reinforcing; and (3) Events that have been reinforcing become unavailable. The emergent symptoms of depression are then strengthened by social attention.

The focus of treatment is primarily educational. Thus, homework is a major focus of the treatment. Among the skills trained are the recording and monitoring of problem situations. The focus of this approach is also to ensure that treatment involves time above and beyond therapy sessions and is of considerable importance for promoting generalization.

Other approaches may also be followed to promote generalization. For example, home observations are used by treatment personnel to identify faulty interpersonal communication and the reinforcement patterns that contribute to the patient's depression. Home observation also assists in the specification of treatment goals. The child's or adolescent's initial self-monitoring and home observations are used to arrive at a behavioral analysis of problems and to contract for goals. The focus of treatment is to increase positive social behavior, which should prove useful in increasing self-esteem and the willingness to interact more frequently with others. Contrasted with the cognitive methods, there is greater emphasis on overt activities and the development of specific skills such as social behavior.

THEORETICAL CONTROVERSY

A cognitive and social learning-operant camp have emerged as the primary, empirically based treatments of depression among children and youth.

A recent review by Beidel and Turner (1986) cogently presents the operant and social learning view. It is argued that the primary differences between these and the cognitive methods are not at the procedural level, although they are evident here. Rather, the major differences are in the conceptualization of psychopathology and basics of the theory (Mahoney & Kazdin, 1979). Beidel and Turner point out that cognitions are not alien to either theoretical camp. The approaches, according to these authors, differ in that operant and social learning camps classify cognitive activities, such as perception and ideation, as private behavioral events. Rather than being phenomena functioning outside the laws of learning, cognitions are seen as other behaviors subject to the same laws of acquisition as more overt events. Cognitive psychologists tend to view many of these internal events as biologically determined and unresponsive to the laws of learning. The thought patterns of a schizophrenic serve as one example (Mahoney, 1974). Operant and social learning approaches emphasize that attentional and/or perceptual distortions of emotionally disturbed persons often result from prior learning history. Individuals who previously have been rewarded for perceiving situations in a negative light are more likely to perceive a new situation in a similar manner. There is evidence that these procedures follow the laws of learning with covert behaviors such as attention and perception improved by utilizing learning theory principles (Lovaas, Schreibman, Koegel, & Rehm, 1971). The treatments described in this chapter follow this latter model.

SOCIAL SKILLS TRAINING

It was mentioned previously in this book that social skills have been found to be directly related to depression and may be precipitated by a reduction in positive reinforcement, and, in fact, specifically assessing social skills in an overall recommended evaluation battery for childhood depression is suggested. Lewinsohn (1975) has also expressed this opinion and incorporates training of this type in his depression treatment package. It is assumed that the depressed person cannot control the interpersonal environment and corresponding emotional reactions of anger or dysphoria. Assessment research has also linked these two areas in research with children (Helsel & Matson, 1984). Many symptoms of depression are social in nature including eye contact, initiating interactions, making appropriate content in speech, smiling, being well groomed and using appropriate tone of speech. These discrete behaviors are usually treated in small clusters of three to five.

Several standard procedures are involved in this form of training. They include instructions, modeling, role playing, performance feedback, social reinforcement, and tangible reinforcement of discrete behaviors. Typically, these procedures occur in one-to-one client-to-therapist training sessions. However, small groups of four to six children may be trained using one or two therapists if children are grouped homogeneously in terms of skill level and type of problem. Generally, five to ten vignettes are used that describe real life episodes of the client. The purpose of training is to enhance skills via practice and reinforcement of appropriate interpersonal behaviors. A typical scene includes:

Narrator Description: You want to play with the other children on the playground but you are afraid they will refuse or that you will mess up and look foolish. You think about it for awhile and decide to approach the children. You do so and one of the children says:

Role-Model Prompt: Hi Sue, would you like to jump rope with us?

Based on the child's response to the role played situation she would be praised for doing well and given feedback in areas where improvement was needed. The therapist might say, "You make good eye contact and made a very pleasant comment to the other child, Sue. However, you spoke so softly that I could barely hear you. Next time it would be great if you would talk louder. Lets try it again."

The role playing might be enhanced further by using a second child to act out the situation, conducting part of the analogue training on the playground where the event had occurred or using other devices to enhance the reality of the training. Modeling would include a demonstration for the child of how to carry out the skill. Typically a tangible reward such as candy, soda, or other treats would be given to the child at the conclusion of training. This approach serves to further motivate the child and is given for "doing your best." Additionally, it allows the child to end the session on a positive note which hopefully will also improve affect. Self-monitoring of specific behaviors or homework in the form of asking the child to carry out three to five tasks, such as initiating a conversation, might be required prior to the next session. Sessions are typically held two to four times a week for 30–40 minutes, and may involve curricular changes so that social skills training sessions could be included as a group activity for the class. If this latter method occurs, it should be coordinated with efforts of the therapist to ensure similarity of target behaviors and staff training procedures. Homework is typically reviewed at the outset of the following session to ensure that the task has been completed and to review what has been done correctly and what requires further improvement.

Several studies have been conducted using variations of this model with depressed children. Calpin and Cincirpini (1978) effectively treated two depressed inpatient children with this approach as did Calpin and Kornblith (1978) with four hospitalized depressed, aggressive children. These two paper presentations were supported by the first published paper on the topic by Matson and his colleagues (Matson et al., 1980). They treated four emotionally disturbed inpatient children, two males and two females from 9 to 11 years of age. The presenting problems of the children included somatic complaints, antisocial behavior, and poor school adaptation. Social skills were assessed using the vignette system described above. Behaviors targeted for intervention included verbal content and appropriate body posture. Intervention involved instructions, information feedback, role playing and social reinforcement for appropriate performance of the target behaviors elicited during vignettes. The children were trained in a group on individually assessed scenes written on a 3″ × 5″ cards read to the youths to facilitate a response from the child engaging in the role play. Feedback was provided by the therapist based on the appropriateness of the child's response and modeling of appropriate behavior was conducted by the therapist when needed. Children improved in training vignettes and perhaps more importantly in vignettes that had not been trained. These results are depicted in Figures 5-1 and 5-2. These findings suggest that children can employ what they have learned in unique ways. Moreover, gains were maintained at a 15-week follow-up. This training program also was replicated with a 10-year-old inpatient boy (Frame, Matson, Sonis, Fialkov, & Kazdin, 1982). The mother completed the CDI, CBC, and BID. Uniformly high rates of depression were evident on all these scales. A naive observer rated the videotape interview, scoring the child as high on depression

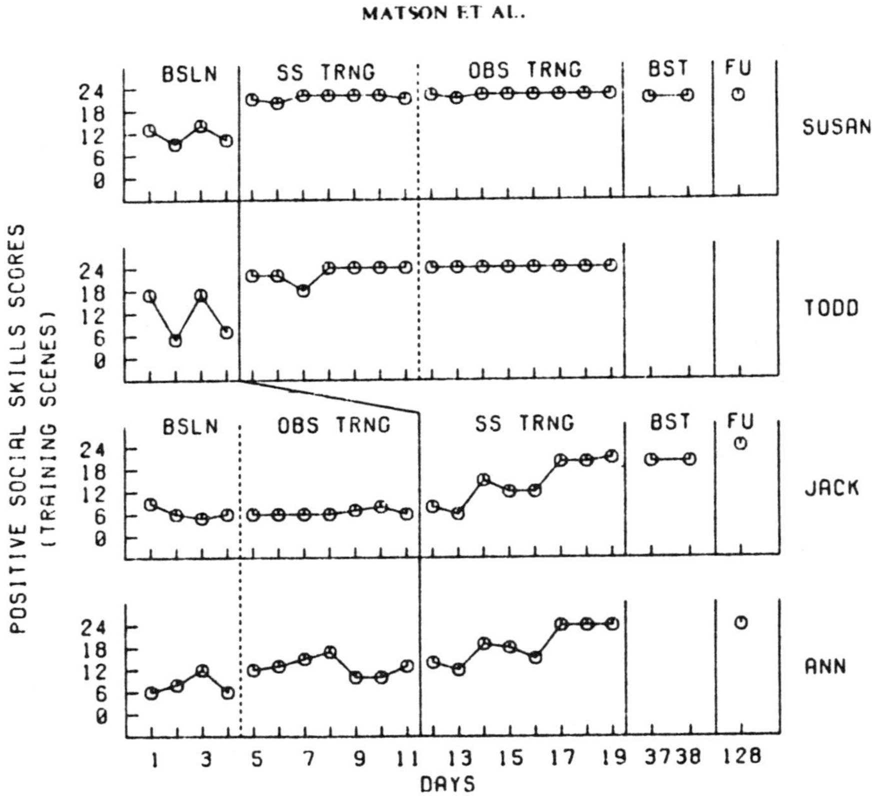

FIGURE 5–1. Frequency of positive social responses on role play scenes directly treated across children and experimental conditions (from Matson et al., 1980). Copyright 1980, by the Association of Behavior Therapy. Reprinted by permission of the publisher and the author.

using the CDI. Behaviors targeted for intervention included inappropriate body position, poor eye contact, poor speech quality, and bland affect. Using the same training procedures described by Matson et al. (1980), marked improvements were evident with continued, although incomplete, improvement evident at an eight-week follow-up.

Schloss, Schloss, and Harris (1984) have also treated depressed young persons. Their clients ranged in age from 15 to 18 and were all diagnosed as schizoaffective. Social skills training included teaching these youths to talk politely in school with the goal of increasing the frequency of appropriate greetings toward other persons. Social responsiveness improved although no major change in the schizoaffective disorder was noticeable. These data suggest that a treatment strategy of this type may

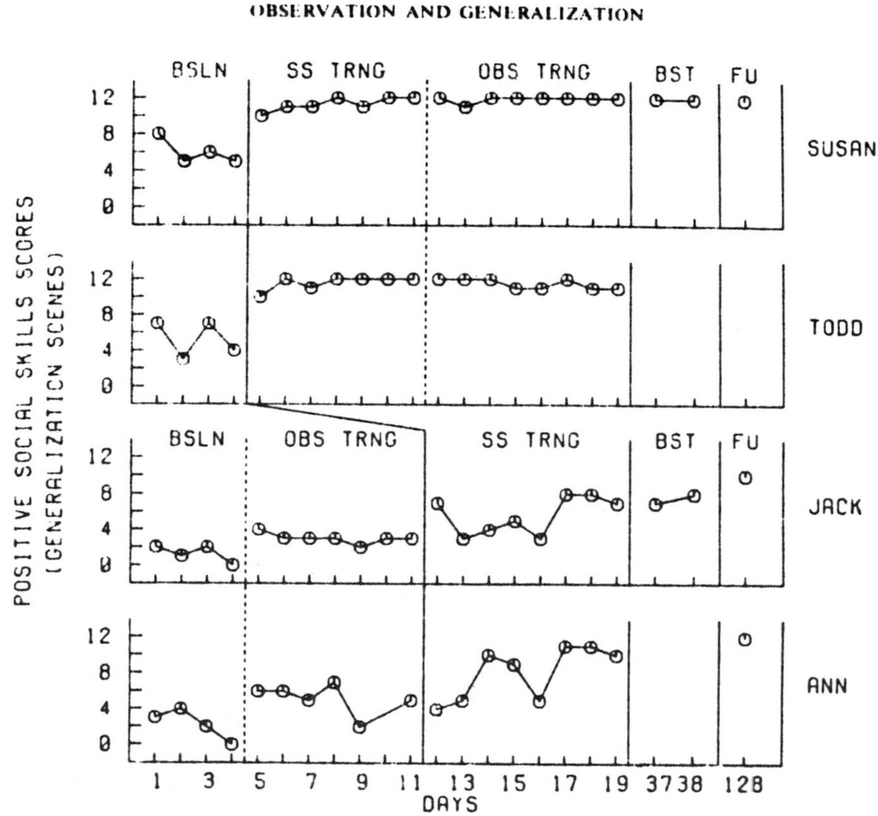

FIGURE 5–2. Frequency of positive social responses on role play scenes which were not treated across children and experimental conditions (from Matson et al., 1980). Copyright 1980, by the Association for Advancement of Behavior Therapy. Reprinted by permissionof the publisher and the author.

have some utility with this treatment population. However, it obviously would not serve as a comprehensive treatment program. Rather, it may be viewed as one component of a more extensive treatment approach that might involve medication, psychotherapy, vocational training, and the development of other necessary independent living and coping skills.

A final social-learning-oriented study to be reviewed was by Fantuzzo, Stovall, Schachtel, Goins, and Hall (1987). Since they treated six children, 3 to 4 years of age, who had been abused by their parents, one might view this as a preventative treatment for those likely to develop depressive symptoms in later life. Such efforts are important since they may head off more serious problems later and can be viewed as a means of decreasing human pain and suffering. Also, it should be pointed out that these treatment procedures might also prove to be effective for older children evincing symptoms of depression. A brief review of their procedures follows.

Prior to the treatment sessions, the two higher-functioning peer-initiators received four 20-minute training sessions during which they taught a variety of play overtures to their withdrawn playmates. These children received training via role playing using the therapist to demonstrate a number of appropriate positive motor and verbal initiations. Next, the therapist had the children practice making initiations with him. These trained children practiced target behaviors with two children selected from their class. The therapist then left the room, but a bug-in-the-ear device was employed between the therapist and the student-helper who had received the prior training. Prompts and reinforcement were given to the student-helper during play sessions until active positive social interactions between these children and the other children in the play environment occurred. This procedure was followed for each training session. In addition, prior to each play period, the student-helper was reminded by the trainer that it was time for him or her to do his special job of inviting the other children to play. Several previously taught strategies would then be reviewed with the student helper. After training sessions, the helper received verbal praise and tangible reinforcers contingent on emitting a fixed daily criterion of at least 10 positive social initiations during each play session. If the student-helper fell below the established criterion, he or she received additional prompting and a booster training session prior to the next session on the following day. As with the other training procedures described in this chapter, this treatment proved to be highly effective. Figures 5-3 and 5-4 exemplify the effectiveness of the program. Figure 5-3 shows the daily number of positive social interactions in treatment (solid circles) and generalization from the treatment setting to the classroom (open circles). Figure 5-4 also provides interesting information – the number of positive social interactions and positive social responses in treatment (solid bar) and generalization (checked bar) settings for each experimental phase. The *A* signifies baseline, *B* denotes treatment and *F-UP* stands for follow-up.

The use of another child in this case was significant for several reasons. First, this type of treatment can be beneficial not only to the child being trained but to the trainer as well, who can learn how to better interact with others. Second, it is useful for increasing generalization, since persons involved in treatment will have many additional opportunities to interact with the client. Third, time savings are provided for therapists, since treatment, at least to some degree, is provided by the individual who aids in the treatment. Other efforts that involve the child's parents as ther-

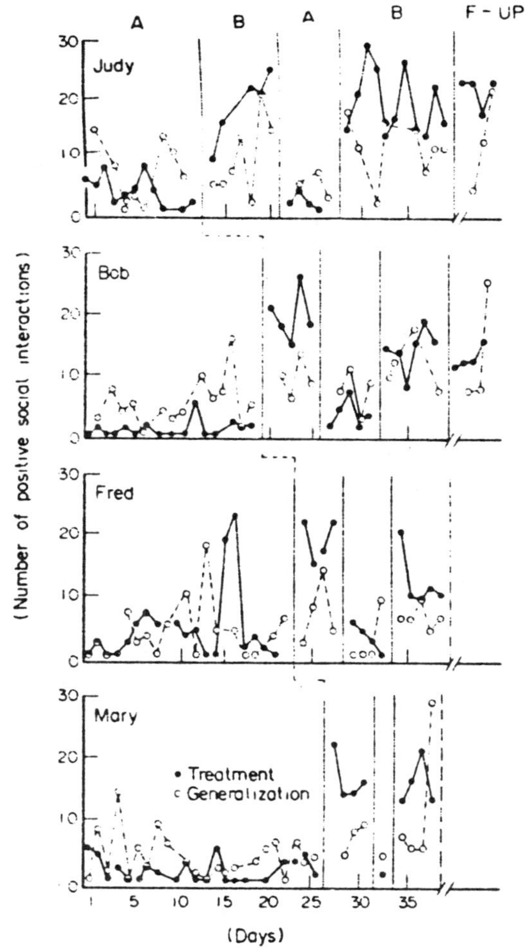

FIGURE 5-3. Daily number of positive social interactions in treatment (solid circle) and generalization (open circle) settings across experimental phases. *Journal of Behavior Therapy and Experimental Psychiatry, 18,* 357–363. Reprinted by permission.

apists or the child as a self-therapist via self-control methods are also options that are means the clinician may wish to consider in the development of a treatment plan.

Social skills training has demonstrated viability for treating depression in children. Obviously, there have not been a great number of studies conducted to date using these training strategies. However, those studies that have appeared evince the utility of this training method with a variety of target behaviors of clients from mild to very severe depressive disorders. Thus, it is a highly recommended approach for childhood

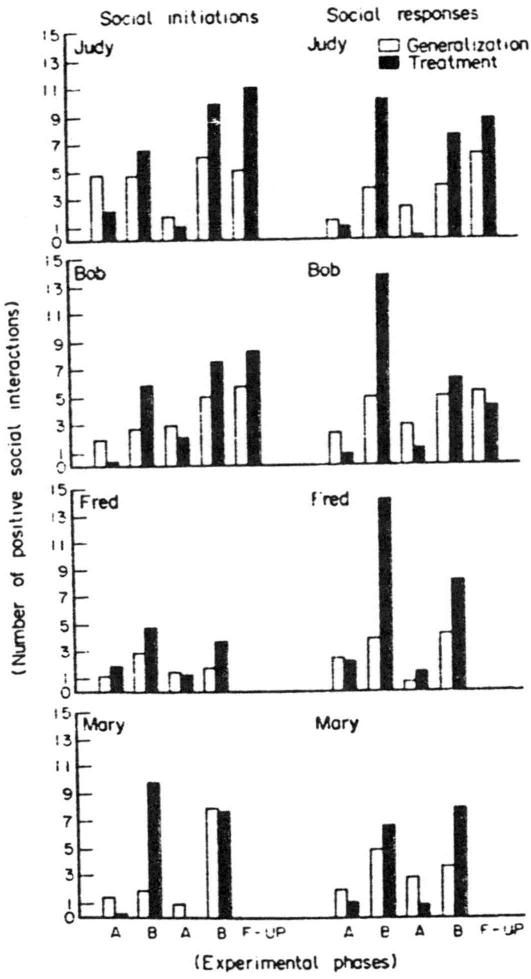

FIGURE 5-4. Mean number of positive social imitations and positive social responses in treatment (solid bar) and generalization (open bar) settings for each experimental phase. *Journal of Behavior Therapy and Experimental Psychiatry, 18,* 357–363. Reprinted by permission.

depression. To further embellish the potential utility and application of social skills training, two hypothetical sample cases will now be presented.

Sample Case

Tim was a 9-year-old boy who had been referred for treatment due to social withdrawal. Assessment consisted of an interview with Tim, his teacher and mother, and the completion of the Child Behavior Checklist and the Matson Evaluation of Social Skills with Youngsters. Data from these measures indicated elevated scores on depression and a number of specific social interpersonal behaviors. The problem was studied further by direct observation of Tim at recess and in the classroom. Based on these observations, checklist data, and discussions, it became apparent that Tim was unhappy because he felt isolated and because he had considerable difficulty making friends, having moved to his new school only three months earlier. The focus of treatment was on teaching discrete skills that would assist Tim in making friends with others.

Role play situations (20 in all) were developed based on various situations at school where the child might initiate positive social interactions with others. These events included asking others to play, sharing with others, and giving assistance to other children. Target behaviors identified for treatment included eye contact, appropriate content of speech, voice tone, and facial affect. Practice began in the therapist's room. When Tim developed proficient skills in this setting, other children were enlisted to practice with Tim in the therapist's room and then on the playground. These efforts, over a period of four months resulted in the development of several friendships for Tim and a dramatic improvement in his previously depressed affect.

Sample Case

Joey was a 10-year-old boy who had been referred to the school psychologist by his teacher. Typically a good student, his performance had dropped off tremendously in the last three months. He had gone from all A's and B's to D's and F's. Most troubling was the fact that he had not been completing homework and did not seem to care about his bad grades. Numerous threats had been made by his parents (e.g., withdrawing a privilege) with no effect. Typically a happy, talkative child, he had become withdrawn and often failed to bother going out to the playground for recess, something which would have been unheard of only a few months before. Other activities, including riding his skateboard and shooting baskets in the driveway at home, had also decreased. He was less verbal than normal and had withdrawn from many social activities.

Joey was interviewed by the psychologist. He was asked to rate various activities he might like to do and a CDI and MESSY were completed. The CDI showed severe levels of depression; major deficits, particularly with respect to social withdrawal, were evident on the MESSY. After school, the psychologist also asked the teacher and Joey's mother to complete the CDI and MESSY. Similar, but even more severe deficits relative to those reported by Joey were evident. It was obvious from the history reported by the mother and noted earlier in this sample cause and via the assessment instruments administered that Joey was experiencing a rather severe case of depression.

The depressive behaviors seemed to be precipitated by the strained relationship between the mother and father. The onset of his problems corresponded to increased arguing between the parents and the movement of his father to an apartment.

The treatment plan consisted of several components aimed at increasing pleasurable activities at school and home. These included role playing social responses to increase the child's proficiency in positive interpersonal behaviors, a major problem area for Joey. Situations were developed and acted out with discrete target responses such as appropriate verbalizations, eye contact, and appropriate facial affect. Treatment consisted of light sessions over a four-week period with a session including the mother to review developments at sessions four and eight. At this point, the emphasis shifted to the home with once a week meetings involving the school psychologist, mother, and Joey to review the week's activities. The target behaviors were reviewed and trained with the school psychologist, at home, and on outings with the mother. She kept a daily log of activities Joey was to engage in and which were likely to be positive ones for him. The mother reviewed the daily log of activities Joey was to engage in and which were likely to be positive ones for him. The mother reviewed the daily log for 10 minutes with Joey early in the evening. For example:

Mother: We had your friend Timmy over to play. Remember we talked about thanking him for coming and letting him choose first the game he would like to play. What happened?

Joey: I did like you said, Mom. I told him to choose first, and he wanted to use my battery-powered car.

Mother: Then what happened?

Joey: He was real happy when I told him that would be okay.

Mother: What other games did you play?

Joey: We played with transformers, my G.I. Joe airplane and watched a Charlie Brown show on our tape player.

Mother: Did you have a good time?

Joey: Yes, we had fun, and Timmy asked if I could come and play some time.

Mother: Good! I also want to tell you, you have been doing a very good job looking at me while you have been talking. Also, you have done a nice job talking about what you did, and you are smiling. That makes Mom very happy. Let's talk about some fun things that we can do tomorrow. I talked with your dad today and one thing for sure is that you can go over to his house for dinner tomorrow night.

This procedure was effective over time, improving Joey's affect at home with some generalization to the school. School behavior was improved further by the teacher who was to ensure that she made at least 10 positive statements to Joey daily. When possible, target behaviors were to be reinforced. The social-skills approach proved to be highly effective.

OPERANT CONDITIONING

The tradition of learning-based treatment approaches is no better exemplified than by the operant methods evolving from the basic research of B. F. Skinner and others. Many childhood conditions have been effectively treated using this methodology. Among these have been social skills (Matson & Fee, in press), aggression (White, Nielsen, & Johnson, 1972), and other emotional problems, and many self-help skills (Hersen & Van Hasselt, 1987).

Operant approaches are defined within a framework of positive reinforcement, negative reinforcement, and punishment. These constructs are aptly described elsewhere (Wielkiewicz, 1986). A variety of procedures is likely to be useful for the treatment of childhood depression, including social and tangible reinforcers, time-out, shaping, chaining, and fading procedures. Given the utility of these methods for a large number of other problem behaviors, it should be easy to adapt some of these strategies for the depressed youngster, and they are likely to be particularly useful for very young or intellectually handicapped children.

Operant conditioning assumes a more structured approach with less responsibility on the part of the client relative to the other treatment methods that have been reviewed in this book. Also, the focus on discrete and discernible behaviors is greater. Given the longer tradition for using operant versus social and cognitive treatments, it is more likely that staff will be available who have some general understanding of the treatment principles. However, it is also true that the successful utilization of this method will require more staff and parent time and participation relative to other behavioral methods as a general rule. The treatment is external versus internal in orientation.

No research specific to depression is available with these treatments. However, a good deal of research on training social skills, which would also be appropriate for depression, exists; they are reviewed with the idea that application to depressed children would be plausible. With minor adaptations, this approach would be appropriate for depressed persons. The primary differentiation of this approach relative to social-learning-oriented training is the use of modeling, verbal feedback, and role play scenes, which are the hallmark of the latter strategy. A few examples with children are provided to exemplify this trend.

Stokes, Baer, and Jackson (1974) treated four mentally retarded children 10–13 years of age using an operant approach. Hand waving was chosen as a positive social greeting, with each child being approached when they were either standing or sitting. Therapist contact lasted for 10 seconds or until greeting responses from the child were given. Approximately 20 daily contacts in the child's natural environment were made. A spontaneous wave by a child resulted in delivery of a tangible reinforcer (e.g., potato chips). Social reinforcers included a smile or hello by the trainer along with a nonverbal contact such as a pat on the shoulder. The greeting response was trained very rapidly with dramatic improvements in this assertive interactive skill.

Jackson and Wallace (1974), in another study of this type, treated a 15-year-old girl for extreme social withdrawal. She would not initiate social interactions and when asked a question would typically answer with a shrug of her shoulders or a nod of her head. Her treatment focused on increasing speech volume, although the methods employed could be used for a range of other responses associated with increasing the number of pleasant and successful interactions and, therefore, hopefully decreasing depression. The authors characterized one aspect of their training program as shaping sessions. The client wore a microphone lavaliere around her neck and word cards, which she was to read, were placed in front of her on a table. A cue light signaled the beginning of a 5-second interval during which the child read the cards, with a 2-second interval between trials. The cue light went on after the session in which she read to the experimenter for 10 minutes. Sessions of 100 words occurred once or twice daily. Training was also provided in the classroom.

A volume meter was employed, and when the child spoke in a louder voice she received a token (poker chip). The tokens could be exchanged at a later point in time for books, beauty aids, and other preferred items. The program proved to be highly effective in enhancing audible speech.

Whitman, Mercurio, and Caponigri (1970) also treated mentally retarded children. These two children were socially withdrawn. Training occurred in 30 sessions wherein food and praise were delivered contingent upon the children's mutual participation in play. Other children were brought into the training situation to facilitate generalization which did occur with children not directly treated.

More recently, Osnes, Guevremont, and Stokes (1987) treated a 4½-year-old girl directly in the classroom setting. The target for intervention was increased peer-directed talk. Prior to play periods, she was verbally prompted to interact with other children. If she met the criteria established for her during the 15-minute observation period, she was taken aside by the trainer during the observation period and given specific praise and affection. Also, she was able to pick a slip of paper from the "happy sack" which named an attention or activity consequence she would receive (e.g., piggyback ride, getting tossed in the air). If she had not reached the criterion number of talks during the observation, she was informed that, "You said you were going to talk a lot today in play but you didn't, so you can't pick from the Happy Sack. You have to sit out." She was then taken to a chair where she had to sit for three minutes. There is one note of caution here. While this treatment proved to be effective and an aversive consequence was necessary, something other than removal from the group may be desirable. This latter contingency is in direct contrast with the goal of decreased withdrawal and from that standpoint may not prove to be the best contingency for depressed children. However in this instance, it appears that the child enjoyed proximity with her classmates, especially after training was initiated. There were marked improvements due to treatment, and these are reflected in Figure 5-5. This figure presents the percentage of intervals talking to and being in the proximity of peers during play which were rated per minute of hand raising during the classroom/large group meetings. The *B* phase here is baseline followed by *CT* for correspondence training with (−) time-out and without (+). The authors do conclude that correspondence training without the aversive component may not always prove to be effective.

Mansdorf (1986), in the treatment of a 10-year-old boy who was socially withdrawn, combined operant and cognitive methods of training. An effort was made to increase class participation by volunteering, initiating social interactions and other assertive acts. Operant training procedures described by the author included social reinforcement via praise by mother when a positive behavior was noted. The other aspect of training, which included a self-control component where responses such as asking to join in with others in playing soccer, were employed. Training sessions of one hour per week were conducted and focused on training assertion skills. Self-instructional training was emphasized using positive statements such as "I could say just what I want to say" and "I'm just as good as Nate. I'll tell him first how I feel." The notion was to have him repeat such statements to himself, and by so doing create a more positive cognitive attitude. With respect to this latter behavioral treatment approach, it was further strengthened and encouraged by feedback, support, and encouragement from his mother.

The most common of the behavioral methods for depression in children is probably social learning. In addition, operant methods would seem to have some utility. And, as demonstrated by the last study that was reviewed here, cognitive methods might prove beneficial when combined with social learning or operant methods. More combinations of this type are likely to appear in the experimental literature and are endorsed for clinical use. For some adolescents with extreme depression,

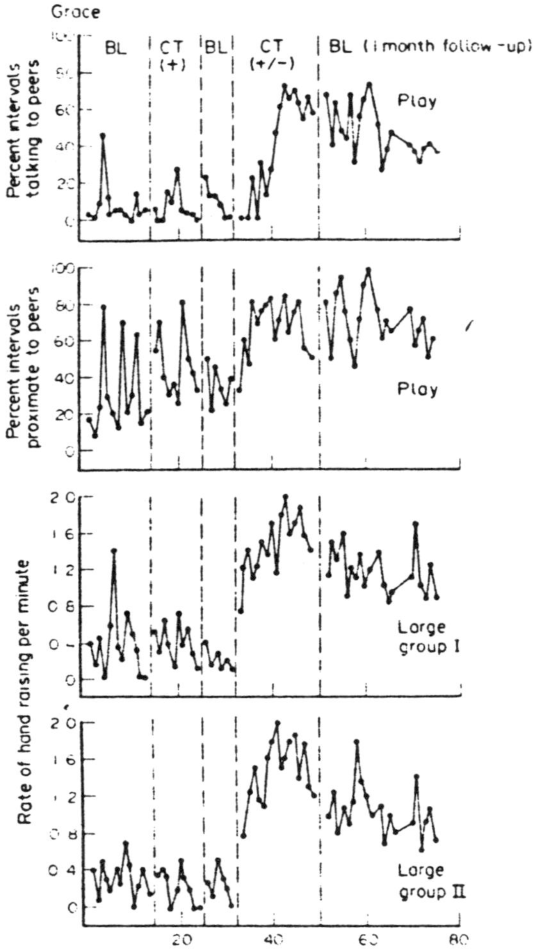

FIGURE 5–5. The percentage of intervals talking to and proximal to peers during play and rate per minute of hand raising during large groups.

drug therapy may also be part of the treatment package. A brief review of this area follows.

DRUGS

Manic-depressive psychosis is rarely seen in children. Thus, Lithium, the drug typically used to treat this problem is infrequently prescribed for children and therefore is not discussed here. Unipolar depression on the other hand is the principal focus of this book. The most common drug group for treating these problems are the tricyclic antidepressants. These medications have received some attention with children and have been used not only with depression but also with panic attacks (Klein, Gittleman, Quitkin, & Rifkin, 1980), enuresis (Blackwell & Currah, 1973), hyperactivity (Rapoport, Quinn, Bradbard, Riddle, & Brooks, 1974), separation anxiety (Gittleman-Klein, 1975), certain types of seizures (Fromm, Wessel, Glas, Alvin, & Van Horn, 1978) and anorexia nervosa (Needleman & Waber, 1977). Several tricyclics have been used, but imipramine seems to be the most popular followed by amitriptyline. In adolescents, the appropriate amount is 75 to 200 mg/day which is often administered in a single dosage at night. The onset of antidepressant effect is not immediate, and typically several weeks are required to determine treatment effectiveness. Blood levels may therefore be evaluated, a procedure that tends to be expensive; many smaller mental health centers do not have the necessary facilities to evaluate blood samples. Therefore, this may prove to be quite expensive. While imipramine has been used to treat this condition (Petti & Law, 1982; Puig-Antich, 1982), amitriptyline has also been tested with children as previously noted and purportedly has fewer side effects (Kashani, Shekim, & Reid, 1984). Currently, the FDA has not approved the use of these and other drugs in their class for children under 12 years of age. And, many believe that such medications should not be used with children due to their many and potentially quite serious side effects (Kaslow & Rehm, 1983). Because of side effects and the general concern about the use of medication with children this is one of the least studied and easily the most controversial of the treatments for unipolar depression in children. In addition, questions can be raised concerning the provision of powerful medication to a child or adolescent who is displaying suicidal ideation or behavior. There is likely to be a place for this approach. However, much research is needed and further review and discussion, by experts in the area, about the role of medications for the treatment of childhood depression will be necessary.

SUMMARY

This chapter has presented a brief review of operant, social learning, and drug approaches to the treatment of depression in children and youth. The social learning package, in particular, is likely to be of use and of considerable interest for those treating depression in children. Also, the social learning package has, along with the cognitive behavioral procedures, the best empirical support of available methodsto this point.

Additionally, there are far fewer objections to this method relative to medication, due to the adverse side effects that are likely to occur with the latter method.

It should also be emphasized that none of the psychological interventions described are totally separate from one another with respect to the treatment components employed. Operant and various aspects of social learning, treatment, or various other combinations of cognitive behavioral interventions are possible. It is suggested, however, that it is perhaps best to have at least one approach as the central or dominant method for a particular client, and, then, relevant subcomponents of other treatment packages might then be added.

Client and family participation in the development, monitoring, and execution of the treatment plan are also of importance no matter what the treatment. Such an emphasis will result in greater support by the child, parent, and school personnel, thus enhancing the likelihood of a successful intervention. It cannot be stressed too strongly that generalization and maintenance of skills is of extreme importance. Therefore, the classic approach involving the therapist providing the treatment in a therapy session is not a viable model any longer as a sole treatment package. It is extremely important to work on needed skills and activities in the school, at home, and in the community at large. Psychological support by the therapist, parent(s), teacher, and any additional important others is a critical aspect of effective intervention for depression. Hopefully, some of the information in this book will prove beneficial in better identifying and treating what is now considered a major emotional problem in childhood.

References

Achenbach, T. M. (1978a). The child behavior profile: I. Boys aged 6 through 11. *Journal of Consulting and Clinical Psychology, 46,* 478–488.

Achenbach, T. M. (1978b). Psychopathology of childhood: Research problems and issues. *Journal of Consulting and Clinical Psychology, 46,* 759–776.

Achenbach, T. M. & Edelbrock, C. S. (1979). The Child Behavior Profile: II. Boys aged 12–16 and girls aged 6–11 and 12–16. *Journal of Consulting and Clinical Psychology, 47,* 223–233.

American Psychiatric Association. (1987). *Diagnostic and Statistical Manual III-R.* Washington, D.C.

Andreasen, N. C. (1982). Affective disorders: Concepts, classification and diagnosis. In E. S. Paykel (Ed.), *Handbook of affective disorders.* New York: Guilford Press. (pp. 24–42).

Anthony, J. & Scott, P. (1960). Manic depressive psychosis in childhood. *Journal of Child Psychology and Psychiatry, 1,* 52–72.

Arieti, S. & Bemporad, J. (1978). *Severe and mild depression.* New York: Basic Books.

Asarnow, J. R. & Carlson, G. A. (1985). Depression self-rating scale: Utility with child psychiatric inpatients. *Journal of Consulting and Clinical Psychology, 53,* 491–499.

Asarnow, J. R., Carlson, G. A., & Guthrie, D. (1987). Coping strategies, self-perceptions, hopelessness, and perceived family environments in depressed and suicidal children. *Journal of Consulting and Clinical Psychology, 55,* 361–366.

Atkeson, B. M. & Forehand, R. (1981). Conduct disorders. In E. J. Mash and L. G. Terdal (Eds.). *Behavioral assessment of childhood disorders.* New York: Guilford Press.

Beck, A. T. (1963). Thinking and depression: I. Idiosyncratic content and cognitive distortions. *Archives of General Psychiatry, 9,* 324–333.

Beck, A. T. (1967). *Depression: Causes and treatment.* Philadelphia: University of Pennsylvania Press.

Beck, A. T. (1976). *Cognitive therapy and emotional disorders.* New York: International University Press.

Beck, A. T., Rush, A. J., Shaw, D., & Emery, G. (1979). *Cognitive therapy of depression.* New York: Guilford Press.

Beidel, D. C. & Turner, S. M. (1986). A critique of the theoretical bases of cognitive-behavioral theories and therapy. *Clinical Psychology Review, 6,* 177–197.

Bemesderfer, S. & Cohler, B. J. (1983). Depressive reactions during separation period: Individualization and self among children of psychotic depressed mothers. In H. L. Morrison (Ed.), *Children of depressed parents: Risk, identification, and intervention* (pp. 159–188). New York: Brune and Stratton.

Bemporad, J. (1978). Manifest symptoms of depression in children and adolescents. In S. Arieti and J. Bemporad (Eds.), *Severe and mild depression: The psychotherapeutic approach.* (pp. 87–106). New York: Basic Books.

Bemporad, J. & Wilson, A. (1978). A developmental approach to depression in childhood and adolescence. *Journal of the American Academy of Psychoanalysis, 6,* 325–352.

Beres, D. (1966). Superego and depression. In R. Lowenstein, L. Newman, M. Schur, & A. Solnit (Eds.), *Psychoanalysis: A general psychology.* (pp. 479–498). New York: International University Press.

Bettes, B. A. & Walker, E. (1986). Symptoms associated with suicidal behavior in childhood and adolescence. *Journal of Abnormal Child Psychology, 14,* 591–604.

Billings, A. G. & Moos, R. H. (1983). Comparisons of children of depressed and nondepressed parents: A social environmental perspective. *Journal of Abnormal Child Psychology, 11,* 463–486.

Birleson, P. (1981). The validity of depressive disorders and the development of a self-rating scale: A research report. *Journal of Child Psychology and Psychiatry, 22,* 73–88.

Blackwell, B. & Currah, J. (1973). The psychopharmacology of nocturnal enuresis. In I. Kalvin, R. C. MacKeith, and S. R. Meadow (Eds.), *Bladder control and enuresis.* (pp. 231–257). London: Heinemann.

Brody, G. H. & Forehand, R. (1986). Maternal perceptions of child maladjustment as a function of the combined influence of child behavior and maternal depression. *Journal of Consulting and Clinical Psychology, 54,* 237–240.

Brumback, R. A., Dietz-Schmidt, S. G., & Weinberg, W. A. (1977). Depression in children referred to an educational diagnostic center: Diagnosis and treatment and analysis of criteria and literature review. *Journal of Nervous and Mental Disease, 165,* 529–535.

Calpin, J. P. & Cincirpini, P. M. (1978). A multiple baseline analysis of social skills in children. Paper presented at the Midwestern Association for Behavior Analysis, Chicago.

Calpin, J. P. & Kornblith, S. J. (1978). Training aggressive children in conflict resolution skills. Paper presented at the Association for the Advancement of Behavior Therapy, Chicago.

Campbell, S. B. (1983). Developmental perspectives in child psychopathology. In T. H. Ollendick & M. Hersen (Eds.), *Handbook of child psychopathology.* New York: Plenum Press.

Cantwell, D. P. (1983). Depression in childhood: Clinical picture and diagnostic criteria. In D. P. Cantwell and G. A. Carlson (Eds.), *Affective disorders in childhood and adolescence: An update.* (pp. 3–8). New York: SP Medical and Scientific Books.

Carlson, G. A. (1983a). Overview of masked or alternative forms of depression. In D. P. Cantwell and G. A. Carlson (Eds.), *Affective disorders in childhood and adolescence: An update.* New York: SP Medical and Scientific Books.

Carlson, G. A. (1983b). Bipolar affective disorders in childhood and adolescence. In D. P. Cantwell and G. A. Carlson (Eds.), *Affective disorders in childhood and adolescence: An update.* New York: SP Medical and Scientific Books.

Carlson, G. A. & Cantwell, D. P. (1979). A survey of depressive symptoms in a child and adolescent psychiatric population. *Journal of the American Academy of Child Psychiatry, 18,* 587–599.

Carlson, G. A. & Cantwell, D. P. (1980a). A survey of depressive symptoms, syndrome and disorder in a child psychiatric population. *Journal of Child Psychology, Psychiatry and Allied Disciplines, 21,* 19–25.

Carlson, G. A. & Cantwell, D. P. (1980b). A survey of depressive symptoms in a child and adolescent psychiatric population. *Journal of the American Academy of Child Psychiatry, 21,* 19–25.

Carlson, G. A. & Strober, M. (1978). Affective disorder in adolescence: Issues in misdiagnosis. *Journal of Clinical Psychiatry, 39,* 63–66.

Carroll, B. J. (1982). The dexamethasone suppression test for melancholia. *British Journal of*

Psychiatry, 140, 292–304.

Cautela, J. R., & Kastenbaum, R. (1967). A reinforcement survey schedule for use in therapy, training and research. *Psychological Reports, 20,* 1115–1130.

Clark, L., Gresham, F. M., & Elliott, S. N. (1985). Development and validation of a social skills assessment measure: The TROSS-C. *Journal of Psychoeducational Assessment. 4,* 347–358.

Cole, D. A. & Rehm, L. P. (1986). Family interaction patterns and childhood depression. *Journal of Abnormal Child Psychology, 14,* 297–314.

Connors, C. K., Himmelhock, J., Goyette, C. H., Ulrich, R., & Neil, J. F. (1979). Children of parents with affective illness. *Journal of the American Academy of Child Psychiatry, 18,* 600–607.

Coopersmith, S. (1967). *The antecedents of self-esteem.* San Francisco: W. H. Freeman.

Coryell, W. (1987). Shifts in attitudes among psychiatric residents: Serial measures over 10 years. *American Journal of Psychiatry, 144,* 913–914.

Costello, C. G. (1980). Childhood depression: Three basic but, questionable assumptions in the Lefkovitz and Burton critique. *Psychological Bulletin, 87,* 187–190.

Costello, E. J., Edelbrock, C. S., Dulcan, M. K., & Kalas, R. (1984). *Testing of the NIMH Interview Schedule for Children (DISC) in a clinical population. Final report to the Center for Epidemiological Studies, National Institute for Mental Health.* Pittsburgh: University of Pittsburgh.

Cytryn, L. & McKnew, D. (1974). Factors influencing the changing clinical expression of the depressive process in children. *American Journal of Psychiatry, 129,* 149–155.

Cytryn, L., McKnew, D., & Bunny, W. (1980). Diagnosis of depression in children. A reassessment. *American Journal of Psychiatry, 137,* 22–25.

Eddy, B. A. & Lubin, B. (In press). The Children's Depression Adjective Checklist (C-DACL) with emotionally disturbed adolescent boys. *Journal of Abnormal Psychology.*

Eisenbruch, M. (1983). Affective disorders in patients: Impact upon children. In D. P. Cantwell & G. A. Carlson (Eds.), *Affective disorders in childhood and adolescence: An update.* (pp. 276–333). New York: Spectrum.

Ellis, A. (1962). *Reason and emotion in psychotherapy.* New York: Lyle Stuart.

Endicott, J. & Spitzer, R. (1978). A diagnostic interview. *Archives of General Psychiatry, 35,* 837–844.

Extein, I., Rosenberg, G., Pottash, A., & Gold. M. (1982). The dexamethasone suppression test in depressed adolescents. *American Journal of Psychiatry, 139,* 1619–1619.

Fantuzzo, J. W., Stovall, A., Schachtel, D., Goins, C., & Hall, R. (1987). The effects of peer social initiations on the social behavior of withdrawn maltreated preschool children. *Journal of Behavior Therapy and Experimental Psychiatry, 18,* 357–363.

Feighner, J. P., Robins, E., Guze, S. B., Woodruff, R. A., Winokur, G., & Munoz, R. (1972). Diagnostic criteria for use in psychiatric research. *Archives of General Psychiatry, 26,* 57–62.

Finch, A. J., Saylor, C. F., & Edwards, G. L. (1985). Children's Depression Inventory: Sex and grade norms for normal children. *Journal of Consulting and Clinical Psychology, 53,* 424–425.

Forehand, R., & Peed, S. (1979). Training parents to modify noncompliant behavior of their children. In J. Finch, Jr. & P. C. Kendall (Eds.), *Treatment and research in child psychopathology.* New York: Spectrum.

Frame, C. L. & Matson, J. L. (1987). *Handbook of assessment in childhood psychopathology: Applied issues in differential diagnosis and treatment evaluation.* New York: Plenum.

Frame, C., Matson, J. L., Sonis, W., Fialkov, M., & Kazdin, A. (1982). Behavioral treatment of depression in a prepubertal child. *Behavior Therapy and Experimental Psychiatry, 13,* 239–243.

Fromm, G. H., Wessel, H. B., Glas, J. D., Alvin, J. D., & Van Horn, G. (1978). Imipramine in absence and myocolonic-astatic seizures. *Neurology, 28,* 953–957.

Fuchs, C. Z. & Rehm, L. P. (1977). A self-control behavior therapy program for depression. *Journal of Consulting and Clinical Psychology, 45,* 206–215.

Geller, B., Rogel, A., & Knitter, E. (1983). Preliminary data on the dexamethasone suppression test in children with major depressive disorders. *American Journal of Psychiatry, 140,* 620–622.

Gittleman-Klein, R. (1975). Pharmacotherapy and management of pathological separation anxiety. *International Journal of Mental Health, 4,* 255–271.

Green, B. J. (1980). Depression in early adolescence: An exploratory investigation of its frequency, intensity and correlates (Doctoral dissertation, Pennsylvania State University). *Dissertation Abstracts International, 41,* 3890–B.

Gresham, F. M., Elliott, S. N., & Black, F. L. (1986). Factor structure replication and bias investigations of the teacher rating of social skills. Louisiana State University.

Hamilton, M. A. (1960). A rating scale for depression. *Journal of Neurology, Neuroscience and Psychiatry, 23,* 56–61.

Hassanyeh, F. & Davison, K. (1980). Bipolar affective psychosis with onset before age 16: Report of ten cases. *British Journal of Psychiatry, 137,* 530–539.

Hawton, K. & Osborn, M. (1984). Suicide and attempted suicide in children and adolescents. In B. B. Lahey & A. E. Kazdin (Eds.), *Advances in clinical child psychology.* (Vol. 7, pp. 57–107). New York: Plenum Press.

Helsel, W. J. & Matson, J. L. (1984). The assessment of depression in children: The internal structure of the Child Depression Inventory (CDI) and its relationship to the Matson Evaluation of Social Skills with Youngster (MESSY). *Behaviour Research and Therapy, 23,* 289–298.

Herjanic, B. & Campbell, W. (1975). Differentiating psychiatrically disturbed children on the basis of a structured interview. *Journal of the Association of Child Psychology, 5,* 127–134.

Herjanic, B. & Campbell, W. (1977). Differentiating psychiatrically disturbed children on the basis of a structured interview. *Journal of Abnormal Child Psychology, 51,* 127–134.

Hersen, M., Eisler, R., & Miller, P. (1974). An experimental analysis of generalization in assertive training. *Behaviour Research and Therapy, 12,* 295–310.

Hersen, M. & Van Hasselt, V. B. (1987). *Behavior therapy with children and adolescents.* New York: John Wiley.

Hirsch, M., Paez, P., Chambers, W., Davis, M., & Puig-Antich, T. (1980). A test-retest reliability study of the K-SADS-P. Presented at the Annual Meeting of the American Academy of Child Psychiatry. Chicago.

Hollin, S. D., Ierubeis, R., Tuason, V. B., Weimer, M. J., Evans, M. D., & Garvey, M. J. (1979). *Combined cognitive-pharmacotherapy versus cognitive therapy alone and pharmacotherapy alone in the treatment of depressed outpatients: Differential treatment outcome in the CPT project.* Unpublished manuscript.

Jacobsen, E. (1938). *Progressive relaxation.* Chicago: University of Chicago Press.

Jacobsen, R. H., Lahey, B. B., & Strauss, C. C. (1983). Correlates of depressed mood in normal children. *Journal of Abnormal Child Psychology, 11,* 29–40.

Jackson, D. A. & Wallace, R. F. (1974). The modification and generalization of voice loudness in a fifteen-year-old retarded girl. *Journal of Applied Behavior Analysis, 7,* 461–471.

Joffe, R. T. & Offord, D. R. (1983). Suicidal behavior in childhood. *Canadian Journal of Psychiatry, 28,* 57–63.

Kanfer, F. H. (1970). Self-regulation: Research, issues and speculations. In C. Neuringer and J. F. Michael (Eds.), *Behavior modification in clinical psychology.* (pp. 178–220). New York: Appleton-Century-Crofts.

Kanfer, F. H. (1971). The many faces of self-control, or behavior modification changes its focus. In R. B. Stuard (Ed.), *Behavioral self-management.* New York: Brunner/Mazel.

Kasanin, J. & Kaufman, M. R. (1929). A study of the functional psychoses in childhood. *American Journal of Psychiatry, 9,* 307.

Kashani, J. H., Beck, N. C., Hoeper, E. W., Fallahi, C., Corcoran, C. M., McAllister, J. A., Rosenberg, T. K., & Reid, J. C. (1987). Psychiatric disorders in a community sample of adolescents. *American Journal of Psychiatry, 144,* 584–589.

Kashani, J. H. & Carlson, G. A. (1987). Seriously depressed preschoolers. *American Journal of Psychiatry, 144,* 348–350.

Kashani, J. H., Husain, A., Shekim, W. O., Hodges, K. K., Cytryn, L., & McKnew, D. H. (1981). Current perspectives on childhood depression: An overview. *American Journal of Psychiatry, 138,* 143–153.

Kashani, J. H., Shekim, W. O., & Reid, J. C. (1984). Amitriptyline in children with major depressive disorder: A double-blind crossover pilot study. *Journal of the American Academy of Child Psychiatry, 23,* 348–351.

Kaslow, N. & Rehm, L. (1983). Childhood depression. In R. J. Morris and T. R. Kratochwill (Eds.), *The practice of child therapy.* New York: Pergamon Press.

Kaslow, N. J., Rehm, L. P., & Siegal, A. W. (1984). Social-cognitive correlates of depression in children. *Journal of Abnormal Child Psychology, 12,* 605–620.

Kazdin, A. E. (1981). Assessment techniques for childhood depression. *Journal of the American Academy of Child Psychiatry, 20,* 358–375.

Kazdin, A. E., Esveldt-Dawson, K., Sherick, R. B., & Colbus, D. (1985). Assessment of overt behavior and childhood depression among psychiatrically disturbed children. *Journal of Consulting and Clinical Psychology, 53,* 201–210.

Kazdin, A. E., French, N. H., Unis, A. S., Esveldt-Dawson, K., & Sherick, R. B. (1983). Hopelessness, depression, and suicidal intent among psychiatrically disturbed inpatient children. *Journal of Consulting and Clinical Psychology, 51,* 504–510.

Kazdin, A. E., Sherick, R. B., Esveldt-Dawson, K. & Rancurello, M. D. (1985). Nonverbal behavior and childhood depression. *Journal of the American Academy of Child Psychiatry, 24,* 303–309.

Kazdin, A. E., Rodgers, A., & Colbus, D. (1986). The hopelessness scale for children: Psychometric characteristics and concurrent validity. *Journal of Consulting and Clinical Psychology, 54,* 241–245.

Klein, D. F., Gittleman, R., Quitkin, F., & Rifkin, A. (1980). *Diagnosis and drug treatment of psychiatric disorders: Adults and children* (2nd ed.). Baltimore: Williams and Wilkins.

Kovacs, M. (1979). The efficacy of cognitive and behavioral therapies for depression. *American Journal of Psychiatry, 137,* 1495–1501.

Kovacs, M. (1981). Rating scales to assess depression in school-aged children. *Acta Paedopsychiatria, 46,* 305–315.

Kovacs, M. (1983). *The Children's Depression Inventory: A self-rated depression scale for school-aged youngsters.* University of Pittsburgh School of Medicine, Unpublished manuscript.

Kovacs, M. (1985). The Children's Depression Inventory (CDI). *Psychopharmacology Bulletin, 21,* 995–998.

Kovacs, M. & Beck, A. (1977). An empirical-clinical approach toward a definition of childhood depression. In J. Schulterbrandt and A. Raskin (Eds.), *Depression in childhood: Diagnosis, treatment and conceptual models* (pp. 1–25). New York: Raven Press.

Kovacs, M. & Beck, A. T. (1979). Cognitive-affective processes in depression. In C. E. Izard (Eds.), *Emotions in personality and psychopathology.* New York: Plenum.

Kovacs, M., Betof, N. G., Celebre, J. F., Mansheim, Petty, L. R., & Raynak, J. T. (1977). *Childhood depression: Myth or clinical syndrome?* Paper presented at the American Academy of Child Psychiatry Conference, Houston, Texas.

Kovacs, M., Feinberg, T. L., Crouse-Novak, M. A., Paulauskas, S. L., & Finkelstein, R. (1984). Depressive disorders in childhood. *Archives of General Psychiatry, 41,* 229–237.

Kovacs, M., Rush, A. T., Beck, A. T., & Hollin, S. D. (1981). Depressed outpatients treated with cognitive therapy or pharmacotherapy: A one year follow-up. *Archives of General Psychiatry, 38,* 33–39.

Kraepelin, E. (1921). *Manic depressive insanity and paranoia.* Edinburgh: Livingstone.

Kuiper, W.A. (1978). Depression and causal attributions for success and failure. *Journal of Personality and Social Psychology, 3,* 236–246.

Kupfer, D. J. & Foster, F. G. (1972). Interval between onset of sleep and rapid-eye movement sleep as an indicator of depression. *Lancet, 2,* 684–688.

Landolt, A. D. (1957). Follow-up studies on circular manic depressive reactions occurring in the young. *Bulletin of the New York Academy of Medicine, 33,* 65–73.

Lang, M. & Tisher, M. (1978). *Children's Depression Scale.* Melbourne: Australian Council for Educational Research.

Lefkowitz, M. M. & Burton, N. (1978). Childhood depression. *Psychological Bulletin, 85,* 716–726.

Lefkowitz, M. M. & Tesiny, E. P. (1980). Assessment of childhood depression. *Journal of Consulting and Clinical Psychology, 48,* 43–50.

Lefkowitz, M. M. & Tesiny, E. P. (1985). Depression in children: Prevalence and correlates. *Journal of Consulting and Clinical Psychology, 53,* 647–656.

Leon, G. R., Kendall, P. C., & Garber, J. (1980). Depression in children: Parent, teacher, and child perspectives. *Journal of Abnormal Child Psychology, 8,* 221–235.

Lesse, S. (1974). Depression masked by acting out behavior patterns. *American Journal of Psychotherapy, 28,* 352–361.

Lewinsohn, P. M. (1974). A behavioral approach to depression. In R. J. Friedman and M. M. Katz (Eds.), *The psychology of depression: Contemporary theory and research.* Washington: Winston.

Lewinsohn, P. M. (1975). The behavioral study and treatment of depression. In M. Hersen, R. M. Eisler, & P. M. Miller (Eds.), *Progress in behavior modification.* (pp. 19–55). New York: Academic Press.

Lewinsohn, P. M. & Shaffer, M. (1971). The use of home observations as an integral part of the treatment of depression. Preliminary report and case studies. *Journal of Consulting and Clinical Psychology, 37,* 87–94.

Lewinsohn, P. M. & Shaw, D. A. (1969). Feedback about interpersonal behavior as an agent of behavior change: A case in the treatment of depression. *Psychotherapy and Psychosomatics, 17,* 82–88.

Lewinsohn, P. M., Weinstein, M. S., & Alper, T. (1970). A behavioral approach to the group treatment of depressed persons: Methodological contributions. *Journal of Clinical Psychology, 26,* 525–532.

Libet, J., Lewinsohn, P. M., & Javorek, F. (1973). *The construct of social skills: An empirical study of several measures on temporal stability, internal structure, validity, and structural generalizability.* Unpublished manuscript. University of Oregon.

Livingston, R., Reis, C., & Ringdahl, I. (1984). Abnormal dexamethasone suppression test results in depressed and nondepressed children. *American Journal of Psychiatry, 141,* 106–108.

Lovaas, O. I., Schreibman, L., Koegel, R., & Rehm, R. (1971). Selective responding by autistic children to multiple sensory input. *Journal of Abnormal Psychology, 77,* 211–222.

Lubin, B., Dupre, V. A., & Lubin A. W. (1967). Comparability and sensitivity of Set 2 (Lists E, F, and G) of the Depression Adjective Check Lists. *Psychological Reports, 20,* (3, pt. 1), 756–758.

Lubin, B. & Zuckerman, M. (1967). Affective and perceptual-cognitive patterns in sensitivity training groups. *Psychological Reports,* 1967, *21*(2), 365–376.

Mackinnon, R. A. & Michels, R. (1971). *The psychiatric interview in clinical practice.* Philadelphia: W. B. Saunders.

Mahoney, M. J. (1974). *Cognition and behavior modification.* Cambridge, MA: Ballinger.

Mahoney, M. J. & Kazdin, A. E. (1979). Cognitive-behavior modification: Misconception and premature evaluation. *Psychological Bulletin, 86,* 1044–1049.

Mansdorf, I. J. (1986). Assertiveness training in the treatment of a child's tic. *Journal of Behavior Therapy and Experimental Psychiatry, 17,* 29–32.

Matson, J. L., Esveldt-Dawson, K., Andrasik, F., Ollendick, T., Petti, T. H., & Hersen, M. (1980). Direct, observation and generalization effects of social skills training with emotionally disturbed children. *Behavior Therapy, 11,* 522-531.

Matson, J. L. & Fee, V. E. (in press). Social skills Difficulties Among Persons with Mental Retardation. In J. L. Matson and J. A. Mulick (Eds.), (2nd ed.) (in press). *Handbook of Mental Retardation.* New York: Pergamon.

Matson, J. L., Helsel, W. J., & Barrett, R. P. (1988). Depression in mentally retarded children. *Research in Developmental Disabilities, 9,* 39–46.

Matson, J. L. & Nieminen, G. S. (1987). A validity study of measures of depression, conduct disorder and anxiety. *Journal of Clinical Child Psychology.*

Matson, J. L. & Ollendick, T. H. (1988). *Enhancing children's social skills.* New York: Pergamon Press.

Morrison, H. L. (1983). *Children of depressed parents: Risk, identification and intervention.* New York: Grune and Stratton.

Mullins, L. L., Peterson, L., Wonderlich, S. A., & Reaven, N. M. (1986). The influence of depressive symptomatology in children on the social responses and perceptions of adults. *Journal of Clinical Child Psychology, 15,* 233–240.

Murphy, G. E., Simons, A. D., Wetzel, R. D., & Lustman, P. J. (1984). Cognitive therapy and pharmacotherapy, singly and together, in the treatment of depression. *Archives of General Psychiatry, 41,* 33–41.

Needleman, H., & Waber, D. (1977). The use of amitriptyline in anorexia nervosa. In R. A. Vigersky (Ed.) *Anorexia nervosa.* (pp. 357–362). New York: Raven.

Norvell, N. & Towle, P. O. (1986). Self-report depression and observable conduct problems in children. *Journal of Clinical Child Psychology, 15,* 228–232.

Olsen, T. (1961). Follow-up study of manic-depressive patients whose first attack occurred before the age of 19. *ACTA Psychiatry Scandinavia, 162,* 45–51.

Orvaschel, H., Sholomskas, D., & Weissman, M. M. (1980). *The assessment of psychopathology and behavioral problems in children—A review of scales suitable for epidemiological and research findings (1967–1979).* Final Progress Report to the Center for Epidemiologic Studies, National Institute of Mental Health; Alcohol, Drug Abuse, and Mental Health Administration.

Osnes, P. G., Guevremont, D. C., & Stokes, T. F. (1987). Increasing a child's prosocial behaviors: Positive and negative consequences in correspondence training. *Journal of Behavior Therapy and Experimental Psychiatry, 18,* 71–76.

Palmer, J. O. (1983). *The psychological assessment of children.* New York: John Wiley and Sons.

Panaccione, V. F. & Wahler, R. G. (1986). Child behavior, maternal depression, and social coercion as factors in the quality of child care. *Journal of Abnormal Child Psychology, 14,* 263–278.

Pearce, J. H. (1978). The recognition of depressive disorder in children. *Journal of the Royal Society of Medicine, 71,* 494–500.

Perris, C. (1966). A study of bipolar (manic-depressive) and unipolar recurrent depressive psychoses. *ACTA Psychiatrica Scandinavia, 42,* (Suppl. 194), 1–188.

Peselow, E. D., Baxter, N., Fieve, R. R., & Barouche, F. (1987). The Dexamethasone suppression test as a monitor of clinical recovery. *American Journal of Psychiatry, 144,* 30–34.

Petti, P. T., & Law, W. (1982). Imipramine treatment of depressed children: A double-blind pilot study. *Journal of Clinical Psychopharmacology, 2,* 107–110.

Pfeffer, C. R., Conte, H. R., Plutchik, R., & Jerret, J. (1980). Suicidal behavior in latency-age children: An outpatient population. *Journal of the American Academy of Child Psychiatry, 19,* 703–710.

Pfeffer, C. R., Solomon, G., Plutchik, R., Mizruchi, M. S., & Weiner, A. (1982). Suicidal behavior in latency-age psychiatric patients: A replication and cross validation. *Journal of the American Academy of Child Psychiatry, 21,* 564–569.

Poznanski, E., Cook, S., & Carroll, B. (1979). A depression rating scale for children. *Pediatrics, 64,* 442–450.

Poznanski, E., Cook, S., Carroll, B., & Corzo, H. (1983). Use of the Children's Depression Rating Scale in an inpatient psychiatric population. *Journal of Clinical Psychiatry, 44,* 200–203.

Poznanski, E., Grossman, J., Buchsbaum, Y., Banegas, M., Freeman, L., & Gibbons, R. (1984). Preliminary studies of the reliability and validity of the Children's Depression Rating Scale. *Journal of the American Academy of Child Psychiatry, 23,* 191–197.

Puig-Antich, J. (1982). Major depression and conduct disorder in prepuberty. *Journal of the American Academy of Child Psychiatry, 21,* 118–128.

Puig-Antich, J. (1983). Neuroendocrine and sleep correlates of prepubertal major depressive disorder: Current status of the evidence. In D. P. Cantwell & G. A. Carlson (Eds.), *Affective disorders in childhood and adolescence: An update.* (pp. 211–227). New York: Spectrum Publications.

Puig-Antich, J. & Chambers, W. (1978a). *Schedule for Affective Disorders and Schizophrenia for School-Aged Children* (6–16 years) (Kiddie-SADS), New York: New York State Psychiatric Institute.

Puig-Antich, J. & Chambers, W. (1978b). The Schedule for Affective Disorders and Schizophrenia for School-age Children (Kiddie-SADS). New York State Psychiatric Institute, 1st edition.

Puig-Antich, J., Chambers, W. J., & Tabrizi, M. A. (1983). The clinical assessment of current depressive episodes in children and adolescents: Interviews with parents and children. In D. P. Cantwell and G. A. Carlson (Eds.), *Affective disorders in childhood and adolescence: An update.* New York: SP Medical and Scientific Books.

Quay, H. C. & Peterson, D. R. (1967). *Manual for the Behavior Problem Checklist.* Champaign, IL: Children's Research Center.

Quay, H. C. (1979). Classification. In H. C. Quay and J. S. Werry (Eds.), *Psychopathological disorders of childhood,* 2nd Ed. New York: John Wiley.

Quay, H. C., & Peterson, D. R. (1975). *Manual for the Behavior Problem Checklist.* Unpublished manuscript.

Rapoport, J. L., Quinn, P. O., Bradbard, G., Riddle, K. D., & Brooks, E. (1974). Imipramine and methylphenidate treatments of hyperactive boys. *Archives of General Psychiatry, 30,* 789–793.

Rehm, L. P. (1977). A self-control model of depression. *Behavior Therapy, 8,* 787–804.

Rehm, L. P., Kaslow, N. J., Rabin, A. S., & Willard, R. (1984). *Outcome of self-control, behavior therapy programs for depression with cognitive, behavioral and combined targets.* Houston, TX.

Rehm, L. P., & Kornblith, S. J. (1979). Behavior therapy for depression: A review of recent developments. In M. Hersen, R. M. Eisler and P. M. Miller (Eds.), *Progress in behavior modification.* New York: Academic Press.

Rehm, L. P., Leventon, B. G. & Ivens, C. (1987). Depression. In C. L. Frame and J. L. Matson (Eds.), *Handbook of assessment in childhood psychopathology: Applied issues in differential diagnosis and treatment evaluation.* New York: Plenum Press.

Reynolds, W. M. (1986). A model for the screening and identification of depressed children and adolescents in school settings. *Professional School Psychology, 1,* 117–129.

Reynolds, W. M. (1987). *Reynolds Adolescent Depression Scale.* Odessa, FL: Psychological Assessment Resource, Inc.

Reynolds, W. M., Anderson, G. & Bartell, N. (1985). Measuring depression in children: A multimethod assessment investigation. *Journal of Abnormal Child Psychology, 13,* 513–526.

Reynolds, W. M., & Stark, K. D. (1985). *Procedures for the development of pleasant activity schedules for children.* Unpublished manuscript.

Reynolds, W. M. & Coats, K. I. (in press). A comparison of cognitive-behavioral therapy and relaxation training for the treatment of depression in adolescents. *Journal of Consulting and Clinical Psychology.*

Reynolds, W. M. & Coats, K. I. (1986). A comparison of cognitive-behavioral therapy and relaxation training for the treatment of depression in adolescents. *Journal of Consulting and Clinical Psychology, 54,* 653–660.

Reynolds, W. M. (1987). *Reynolds Adolescent Depression Scale.* Odessa, FL: Psychological Assessment Resource, Inc.

Rimm, D. C., & Masters, J. C. (1979). *Behavior therapy: Techniques and empirical findings.* New York: Academic Press.

Robinson, J. C., & Lewinsohn, P. M (1973). Behavior modification of speech characteristics in a chronically depressed man. *Behavior Therapy, 4,* 150–152.

Rochlin, G. (1959). The loss complex. *Journal of the American Psychoanalytic Association, 7.* 299–316.

Rutter, M. (1986). The developmental psychopathology of depression: Issues and perspectives. In M. Rutter, C. E. Izard and P. B. Read (Eds.), *Depression in young people: Developmental and clinical perspectives.* New York: Guilford Press.

Rutter, M., & Gould, M. (1985). Classification. In M. Rutter & L. Hersov (Eds.), *Child and adolescent psychiatry: Modern approaches.* Oxford: Blackwell Scientific Publications.

Rutter, M., Izard, C. E., & Read, P. B. (1986). *Depression in young people: Developmental and clinical perspectives.* New York: Guilford Press.

Saylor, C. F., Finch, A. J., Jr., Spirito, A., & Bennett, B. (1984). The Children's Depression Inventory: A systematic evaluation of psychometric properties. *Journal of Consulting and Clinical Psychology, 52,* 955–967.

Schloss, P. J., Schloss, C. N., & Harris. L. (1984). A multiple baseline analysis of an interpersonal skills training program for depressed youth. *Behavioral Disorders, 9,* 182–188.

Schwartz, G. E., Fair, P. L., Mandel, M. R. Salt, P., Mieske, M., & Klerman, G. L. (1978). Facial electromyography in the assessment of improvement in depression. *Psychosomatic Medicine, 40,* 355–360.

Schwartz, G. E., Fair, P. L., Salt, P., Mandel, M. R., & Klerman, G. L. (1976a). Facial expression and imagery in depression: An electromyographic study. *Psychosomatic Medicine, 38,* 337–347.

Schwartz, G. E., Fair, P. L., Salt, P., Mandel, M., & Klerman, G. L. (1976b). Facial muscle patterning to affective imagery in depressed and nondepressed subjects. *Science, 192,* 489–491.

Seagull, E. A. W. & Weinshank, A. B. (1984). Childhood depression in a selected group of low-achieving seventh graders. *Journal of Clinical Child Psychology, 13,* 134–140.

Seligman, M. E. P. (1981). A learned helplessness point of view. In L. Rehm (Ed.), *Behavior therapy for depression. Present status and future directions.* New York: Academic Press.

Shaffer, D. (1974). Suicide in childhood and early adolescence. *Journal of Child Psychology and Psychiatry. 15,* 275–291.

Shaw, B. F. (1977). Comparison of cognitive therapy and behavior therapy in the treatment of depression. *Journal of Consulting and Clinical Psychology, 45,* 543–551.

Shectman, A. (1970). Age patterns in children's psychiatric symptoms. *Child Development, 41,* 683–693.

Shoemaker, O. S., Erickson, M. T., & Finch, A. J., Jr. (1986). Depression and anger in third and fourth grade boys: A multimethod assessment approach. *Journal of Clinical Child Psychology, 15,* 290–296.

Smucker, M. R., Craighead, W. E., Craighead, L. W., & Green, B. J. (1986). Normative and reliability data for the Children's Depression Inventory. *Journal of Abnormal Child Psychology, 14,* 25–40.

Sokoloff, R. M. & Lubin, B. (1983). Depressive mood in adolescents, emotionally disturbed females: Reliability and validity of an adjective checklist (C-DACL). *Journal of Abnormal Child Psychology, 11,* 531–536.

Spates, C. R. & Kanfer, F. H. (1977). Self-monitoring, self-evaluation, and self-reinforcement in children's learning: A test of multi-stage self-regulation model. *Behavior Therapy, 8,* 9–16.

Spitzer, R. L. & Endicott, J. (1978). *Schedule for Affective Disorders and Schizophrenia.* NIMH Research Branch, Collaborative Program on the Psychology of Depression, 3rd edition.

Spitzer, R. L., Endicott, J., & Robins, E. (1978). *Research diagnostic criteria for a selected group of functional disorders.* (3rd Ed.) New York: New York State Psychiatric Institute.

Stark, K. D., Reynolds, W. M., & Kaslow, N. J. (1987). A comparison of the relative efficacy of self-control therapy and a behavioral problem-solving therapy for depression in children. *Journal of Abnormal Child Psychology, 15,* 91–113.

Stark, K. D., Reynolds, W. M., & Kaslow, N. J. (in press). A comparison of the relative efficacy of self-control and behavior therapy for the reduction of depression in children. *Journal of Abnormal Child Psychology.*

Stokes, T. F., Baer, D. M., & Jackson, R. L. (1974). Programming the generalization of a greeting response of four retarded children. *Journal of Applied Behavior Analysis, 7,* 599–610.

Strauss, C. C., Forehand, R., Frame, C., & Smith, K. (1984). Characteristics of children with extreme scores on the Children's Depression Inventory. *Journal of Clinical Child Psychology, 13,* 227–231.

Taylor, M. A. & Abrams, R. (1980). Reassessing the bipolar-unipolar dichotomy. *Journal of Affective Disorders, 2,* 195–217.

Tesiny, E. P., Lefkowitz, M. M., & Gordon, W. H. (1980). Childhood depression, locus of control and school achievement. *Journal of Educational Psychology, 72.* 506–510.

Teuting, P., Koslow, S. H., & Hirschfeld, R. M. A. (1982). *Special report on depression research* (DHHS Publication No. ADM 81-1085, National Institute of Mental Health). Washington, DC: U. S. Government Printing Office.

Tharp, R. G. & Wetzel, R. J. (1969). *Behavior modification in the natural environment.* New York: Academic Press.

Tisher, M. & Lang, M. (1983). The Children's Depression Scale: Review and further developments. In D. P. Cantwell and G. A. Carlson (Eds.), *Affective disorders in childhood and adolescence: An update.* New York: SP Medical and Scientific Books.

Tsuang, M. T. (1978). Familial subtyping of schizophrenia and affective disorders. In R. L. Spitzer and O. L. Klein (Eds.), *Critical issues in psychiatric diagnosis.* (pp. 203–211). New York: Raven.

Weinberg, W. A., Rutman, J., Sullivan, L., Penick, E. C., & Dietz, S. G. (1973). Depression in children referred to an educational diagnostic center: Diagnosis and treatment: Preliminary report. *Journal of Pediatrics, 83,* 1065–1072.

Weissman, M. M. & Paykel, E. S. (1974). *The depressed woman.* Chicago: University of Chicago Press.

Weissman, M. M., Prusoff, B. A., Gammon, G. D. Merikangas, K. E., Leckman, J. F., & Kidd, K. K. (1984). Psychopathology in children (ages 6–18) of depressed and normal parents. *Journal of the American Academy of Child Psychiatry, 23,* 78–84.

Welner, Z., Welner, A., McCrary, D., & Leonard, M. A. (1977). Psychopathology in children of inpatients with depression: A controlled study. *Journal of Nervous and Mental Disease, 164,* 408–413.

Wetzel, R. D., Margulies, T., Davis, R. & Karam, E. (1980). Hopelessness, depression, and suicide intent. *Journal of Clinical Psychiatry, 41,* 159–160.

Whatmore, G. B. & Kohli, D. (1968). Dysponesis: A neurophysiologic factor in functional disorders. *Behavioral Science, 13,* 102–104.

White, G., Nielsen, G., & Johnson, S. (1972). Time-out duration and the suppression of deviant behavior in children. *Journal of Applied Behavior Analysis, 5,* 111–120.

Whitman, T. L., Mercurio, J. R., & Caponigri, V. (1970). Development of social responses in two severely retarded children. *Journal of Applied Behavior Analysis, 3,* 133–138.

Wielkiewicz, R. M. (1986). *Behavior management in the schools: Principles and procedures.* New York: Pergamon.

Williams, J. G., Barlow, D. H., & Agras, W. S. (1972). Behavioral measurement of severe depression. *Archives of General Psychiatry, 27,* 330–333.

Willner, P. (1985). *Depression: A psychological synthesis.* New York: John Wiley and Sons.

Wirt, R. D., Lachar, D., Klinedurst, J., & Seat, P. D. (1977). *Multidimensional descriptions of child personality: A manual for the Personality Inventory for Children.* Los Angeles: Western Psychological Services.

Wolpe, J. (1982). *The practice of behavior therapy* (3rd ed.). New York: Pergamon Press.

Author Index

Abrams, R., 12
Achenbach, T. M., 12, 55, 58
Agras, W. S., 33
Alvin, J. D., 91
American Psychiatric Association, 2
Anderson, G., 44
Andrasik, F., 79
Andreason, N. C., 1
Anthony, J., 7, 12
Arieti, S., 10, 11
Asarnow, J. R., 49, 52
Atkeson, B. M., 35

Baer, D. M., 87
Banegas, M., 47
Barlow, D. H., 33
Barouche, F., 37
Barrett, R. P., 43
Bartell, N., 44
Baxter, N., 37
Beck, A. T., 41, 58, 64, 68, 69, 74
Beck, N. C., 9
Bemesderfer, S., 16
Bemporad, J., 10, 11, 17
Bennett, B., 42
Bereas, D., 2
Betof, N. G., 42
Bettes, B. A., 11
Billings, A. G., 13, 16
Birleson, P., 49, 58
Black, F. L., 53
Blackwell, B., 91
Bradbard, G., 91
Brody, G. H., 13
Brooks, E., 91
Brumback, R. A., 6
Buchsbaum, Y., 47
Bunny, W., 9
Burton, N., 8

Calpin, J. P., 79
Campbell, S. B., 26
Campbell, W., 31
Cantwell, D. P., 1, 9, 17, 41, 44, 48, 58
Caponigri, V., 88
Carlson, G. A., 9, 12, 14, 41, 44, 48, 49, 52
Carroll, B. J., 37, 47
Cautela, J. R., 54
Celebre, J. F., 42
Chambers, W., 29, 30, 31
Cincirpini, P. M., 79
Clark, L., 52, 53
Coats, K. I., 65, 69, 72, 74
Cohler, B. J., 16
Colbus, D., 32
Cole, D., 20
Conners, C. K., 16
Conte, H. R., 10
Cook, S., 47
Coryell, W., 15
Corzo, H., 47
Costello, C. G., 14
Costello, E. J., 31
Craighead, L. W., 44
Craighead, W. W., 44
Crouse-Novak, M. A., 51
Currah, J., 91

Cytryn, L., 8, 9, 14

Davis, R., 31, 50
Davison, K., 14
Dietz-Schmidt, S. G., 6
Dulcan, M. K., 31

Edelbrock, C. S., 31, 55, 58
Eddy, B. A., 47
Edwards, G. L., 43
Eisenbruch, M., 20
Eisler, R., 52
Elliott, S. N., 52, 53
Ellis A., 65, 66, 67, 68
Emery, G., 64
Endicott, J., 2, 30
Erickson, M. T., 42
Esveldt-Dawson, K., 6, 32, 58, 70
Evans, M. D., 68
Extein, I., 37

Fallahi, C., 9
Fair, P. L., 38
Fantuzzo, J. W., 81
Fee, V. E., 87
Feighner, J. P., 2, 4, 5, 6
Feinberg, T. L., 51
Fialkov, M., 79
Fieve, R. R., 37
Finch, A. J., 42, 43
Finkelstein, R., 51
Forehand, R., 3, 13, 35
Foster, F. G., 16
Frame, C. L., 3, 32, 79
Freeman, L., 47
French, N. H., 58
Fromm, G. H., 91
Fuchs, C. Z., 35

Gammon, G. D., 16
Garber, J., 56
Garvey, M. J., 69
Geller, B., 37
Gibbons, R., 47
Gittleman-Klein, R., 91
Glas, J. D., 91
Goins, C., 81
Gold, M., 37
Gordon, W. H., 7
Goyette, C. H., 16
Green, B. J., 44
Gresham, F. M., 52, 53
Grossman, J., 47

Guevremont, D. C., 88
Guthrie, D., 52
Guze, S. B., 6

Hall, R., 81
Hamilton, M. A., 47
Harris, L., 80
Hassanyeh, K., 14
Hawton, K., 10
Helsel, W. J., 42, 43, 44, 52, 78
Herjanic, B., 29, 31
Hersen, M., 52, 79, 80
Himmelhock, C. K., 16
Hirsch, M., 31
Hirschfeld, R. M. A., 15
Hodges, K. K., 14
Hoeper, E. W., 9
Hollin, S. D., 68, 69
Hussain, A., 14

Ierubeis, R., 68
Ivens, C., 2, 8
Izard, C. E., 13

Jackson, R. L., 87, 88
Jacobson, R. H., 9, 44
Javorek, F., 34
Jerret, J., 10
Joffe, R. T., 10
Johnson, S., 87

Kalas, R., 31
Kanfer, F. H., 17, 66
Karam, E., 50
Kasanin, J., 14
Kashani, J. H., 9, 14, 91
Kaslow, N. J., 65, 71, 72, 91
Kastenbaum, R., 54
Kaufman, M. R., 14
Kazdin, A. E., 7, 32, 41, 49, 58, 77, 79, 80
Kendall, P. C., 56
Klein, D. F., 91
Klerman, G. L., 38
Klinedurst, J., 56, 58
Knitter, E., 37
Koegel, R., 77
Kohli, D., 38
Kornblith, S. J., 63, 79
Koslow, S. H., 15
Kovacs, M., 41, 42, 43, 44, 58, 63, 68, 69

Kuiper, W. A., 54
Kupfer, D. J., 16

Lacher, D., 56, 58
Lahey, B. B., 9
Landolt, A. D., 14
Lang, M., 45, 46, 58
Law, W., 91
Leckman, J. F., 16
Lefkowitz, M. M., 7, 8, 48, 58
Leon, G. R., 56
Leonard, M. A., 20
Lesse, S., 8
Leventon, B. G., 2, 8
Lewinsohn, P. M., 17, 19, 32, 34, 44, 64, 76, 78
Libet, J., 34
Livingston, R., 37
Lovaas, O. I., 77
Lubin, B., 47, 58
Lustman, P. J., 69

MacKinnon, R. A., 26
Mahoney, M. J., 77
Mandel, M. R., 38
Mansdorf, I. J., 89
Margulies, T., 50
Masters, J. C., 65
Matson, J. L., 9, 32, 42, 43, 44, 52, 58, 78, 79, 80, 87
McAllister, J. A., 9
McCrary, D., 20
McKnew, D., 8, 9, 14
Mercurio, J. R., 88
Merikangas, K. E., 16
Michels, R., 26
Mieske, M., 38
Miller, P., 52
Mizruchi, M. S., 10
Moos, R. H., 13, 16
Morrison, H. L., 13
Mullins, L. L., 20
Munoz, R., 6
Murphy, G. E., 69

Needleman, H., 91
Neil, J. F., 16
Nielsen, G., 87
Nieminen, G. S., 9
Norvell, N., 9

Offord, D. R., 10
Ollendick, T. H., 79, 80
Olsen, T., 14
Orvaschel, H., 42
Osborn, M., 10
Osness, P. G., 88

Paez, P., 31
Palmer, J. O., 28
Panaccione, V. F., 13
Paulauskas, S. L., 51
Paykel, E. S., 19
Pearce, J. H., 13
Peed, S., 35
Penick, E. C., 6
Perris, C., 12
Peselow, E. E., 37
Peterson, D. R., 3, 55
Peterson, L., 20
Petti, P. T., 79, 80, 91
Petty, L. R., 42
Pfeffer, C. R., 10
Plutchik, R., 10
Pottash, A., 37
Poznanski, E., 47, 58
Prusoff, B. A., 16
Puig-Antich, J., 16, 29, 30, 31

Quay, H. C., 3, 55
Quinn, P. O., 91
Quitkin, R., 91

Rabin, A. S., 71
Rancurello, M. P., 7
Rapoport, J. L., 91
Raynack, J. T., 42
Read, P. P., 12
Reaven, N. M., 20
Rehm, L. P., 2, 8, 17, 20, 29, 35, 63, 70, 71, 77, 91
Reid, J. C., 9, 91
Reis, C., 37
Reynolds, W. M., 44, 57, 58, 65, 69, 71, 72, 74
Riddle, K. D., 91
Rifkin, A., 91
Rimm, D. C., 65
Ringdahl, I., 37
Robins, E., 2, 6

Robinson, J. C., 32
Rochlin, G., 2
Rogel, A., 37
Rosenberg, G., 37
Rosenberg, T. K., 9
Rush, A. J., 69
Rutman, J., 6

Salt, P., 38
Saylor, C. F., 42, 43
Schachtel, D., 81
Schloss, C. N., 80
Schloss, P. J., 80
Schreibman, L., 77
Schwartz, G. E., 38
Scott, P., 7, 12
Seagull, E. A. W., 6
Seat, P. D., 56, 58
Seligman, M. E. P., 18
Shaffer, D., 10, 34
Shaw, B. F., 68
Shaw, D., 34
Shectman, A., 11
Shekim, W. O., 14, 91
Sherrick, R. B., 7, 32, 58
Shoemaker, O. S., 42
Sholomskas, D., 42
Simons, A. P., 69
Smith, K., 3
Smucker, M. R., 44
Solomon, G., 10
Sonis, W., 79
Spates, C. R., 66
Spirito, A., 42
Spitzer, R. L., 2, 4, 30
Stark, K. D., 65, 71, 72–73
Stokes, T. F., 87, 88
Stoval, A., 81
Strauss, C. C., 3, 9, 44
Strober, M., 14
Sullivan, L., 6

Tabrizi, M. A., 29
Taylor, M. A., 12
Tesiny, E. P., 7, 48
Teuting, P., 15
Tharp, R. J., 54
Tisher, M., 45, 46, 58
Towle, P. O., 9
Tsuang, M. T., 12
Tuason, V. B., 68
Turner, S. M., 77

Ulrich, R., 30
Unis, A. S., 58
Van Hasselt, B., 87, 88
Van Horn, G., 91

Waber, D., 91
Walker, E., 11
Wallace, R. F., 88
Weimer, M. J., 68
Weinberg, W. A., 5, 6
Weiner, A., 10
Weinshank, A. B., 6
Welner, A., 20
Welner, Z., 20
Weissman, M. M., 16, 19, 42
Wessel, H. B., 91
Wetzel, R. D., 50, 54, 69
Whaler, R. G., 13
Whatmore, G. B., 38
White, G., 87
Whitman, T. L., 88
Wielkiewicz, R. M., 87
Willard, R., 71
Williams, J. G., 33
Willner, P., 11
Wilson, A., 17
Winokur, G., 6
Wirt, R. D., 56, 58
Woodruff, R. A., 6
Wolpe, J., 72
Wonderlich, S. A., 20

Subject Index

Abused children, 81
Academic functioning, 7
Activity scheduling, 64, 65, 68, 73
Adoption studies, 17
Aggression, 7
Alcoholism, 12
Amitryptaline, 91
Anthony and Scott criteria, 7
Antidepressants, 90–91
Anxiety, 3, 72
Assessment, 22–59
Assessment model, 56
Attribution retraining, 90–91

Beck Depression Inventory (BDI), 47
Beck Index of Depression (BID-R), 34, 41, 48, 79
Behavior Problem Checklist, 3, 9, 55
Biochemical measures, 3, 7–38, 39
Biochemistry, 14
Biological theories, 14
Bipolar depression, 11–12, 14
Bug-in-ear device, 82

Chaining, 87
Checklists, 25, 39, 40–59
  self-report, 41–4
Child Behavior Checklist (CBC), 55–56, 73, 79, 84
Child Depression Inventory (CDI), 9, 30, 34, 41–44, 45, 47, 48, 49, 52, 73, 74, 79, 80, 85
Children's Depression Adjective Checklist (D-DACL), 41, 47, 73
Children's Depression Rating Scale (CDRS), 41, 47
Child's Game, 35–36
Child Depression Scale, 41, 45–46
Classification systems, 2–6
Coding systems, 35
Cognitive behavior therapy, 60, 63–73, 76, 77, 87, 89, 91, 92
Cognitive restructuring, 65
Contracting, 70, 77
Coopersmith Self-Esteem Inventory, 58, 73
Correspondence training, 89
Cortisol, 15, 16
Covert behavioral rehearsal, 63
Covert modeling, 60
Covert reinforcement, 60, 66
Course, 27
Cyclothmia, 12

Depression Self-Rating Scale (DSRS), 41, 49
Developmental issues, 12–13, 17, 26
Dexamethasone Suppression Test (DST), 37
Diagnostic systems, 2–6
DSM-II, 2
DSM-III, 2, 4, 6, 31, 32, 33, 44, 55
DSM-III-R, 3, 27, 30, 56, 57
Direct observation (*see* observation)

Electromyography (EMG), 38
Environment, 15, 76
Environmental models, 17–20
Etiology, 15–30

Factor analysis, 3
Fading, 87
Family history, 12, 15, 16
Family therapy, 60
Feedback, 74, 77, 79, 87, 89
Feighner criteria, 2, 4, 5

Generalization, 76, 77, 82, 88
Goal-setting, 70, 74, 77
Growth hormone response, 15, 16

Hearing impaired children, 45
History, 1–2
Homework, 63, 67, 68, 69, 71, 73, 76, 79
Hopelessness Scale, 52
Hypomanic episode, 11

ICD-9, 3
Imipramine, 91
Instructions, 78, 79
Interviews, 25
 structured, 28–32
 unstructured, 26–28

Kiddie-SADS, 29
Kraeplinian model, 2

Learned Helplessness, 17–19, 52
Lewinsohn Model, 52
Lithium, 90

Major Depressive Episode, 11–12
Manic depressive psychosis, 11–12
Masked depression, 7–9
Matson Evaluation of Social Skills with Youngsters (MESSY), 52, 73, 74, 85
Mediator-Reinforcer Incomplete Blank (MRB), 54
Mentally retarded children, 45, 49, 53, 87–88
MHPG, 15
Modeling, 74, 77, 79, 82, 87
Muscle tension, 37

National Institute of Mental Health (NIMH), 14
Negative reinforcement, 87
Nonverbal behavior, 7–8

Observations, 32–37, 76, 85
Operant conditioning, 4, 6, 68, 75, 77, 87–90, 91, 92

Parent behavior, 13, 19–20
Parent's Game, 35
Parent training, 74
Peer-initiators, 82
Peer Nomination Inventory for Depression (PNID), 41, 48
Personality Inventory for Children (PIC), 55
Pharmacological intervention, 69, 81, 90–91, 92
Physiological measures, 37–38, 39
Pleasant Events Schedule (PES), 54
Prevalence, 14–15
Problem-solving, 63, 72–73
Prompts, 82
Psychophysiological measurement, 16
Punishment, 87

Rapport, 25, 27
Rational-Emotive Therapy, 66–68
RDC, 2, 4, 30
Reinforcement, 19, 20, 25, 27, 34, 53, 69, 70, 73, 78, 82, 87, 88, 89
 assessment of, 54–55
Reinforcement Survey Schedule, 54
Relaxation training, 70, 71–72
REM sleep, 16
Reynold's Adolescent Depression Scale (RADS), 9, 41, 44–45, 70
Role playing, 74, 77, 79, 82, 85, 86, 87

SADS (Schedule for Affective Disorders and Schizophrenia), 30
Self-control, 17, 60, 66, 69, 70, 89
Self-evaluation, 65, 66, 69, 70, 71, 74
Self-monitoring, 60, 63, 64, 65, 69, 70, 71, 74, 79
Self-Rating Scale of Depressed Mood, 47
Self-regulation, 17–18
Self-reinforcement, 65, 66, 69, 70, 71, 74
Sex ratio, 13
Shaping, 87, 88
Short Children's Depression Inventory, 41, 48–49
Sleep, 16
Social reinforcement, 76
Social skills, 52, 76, 79, 87, 88, 89
Social skills training, 78–87
Stress, 72
Symptoms, 3–8
Systematic desensitization, 71–72

Time-out, 87, 89
Token reinforcement, 88
Treatment, 60–92
Tricyclic antidepressants, 91
TROSS-C, 52–53

Unipolar depression, 9, 14–15, 19, 64, 76, 90

Vegetative symptoms, 1
Verbal behavior, 32, 34, 35, 79, 80, 85, 86
Vocational training, 81

Withdrawal, 84, 85, 88, 89

Zung, 48

About the Author

Johnny L. Matson is Professor of Clinical Psychology at Louisiana State University in Baton Rouge, Louisiana. In addition to this position he has held academic positions in the Department of Learning and Development at Northern Illinois University and the Departments of Psychiatry and Psychology at the University of Pittsburgh. He has also served as Program Director for the Jemison Center at Partlow State School and Hospital for mentally retarded persons in Tuscaloosa, Alabama.

Dr. Matson has written over 260 published works, including 15 books. The *Handbook of Mental Retardation* won the award for best book in the social and behavioral sciences in 1983 from the American Association of Publishers. He is on the editorial board of several journals including the *Journal of Educational Psychology Behavior Therapy, Journal of Clinical Child Psychology, Mental Retardation, Psychotherapy, Scandinavian Journal of Behavior Therapy* and the *Australian and New Zealand Journal of Developmental Disabilities.* He is also the editor of *Research in Developmental Disabilities* (Pergamon), a merger of *Analysis and Intervention in Developmental Disabilities* and *Applied Research in Mental Retardation.*

Holding national offices in several organizations, he has been coordinator of Membership Affairs for the Association for Advancement of Behavior Therapy and president of Division 33 (Mental Retardation) of the American Psychological Association. His research interests include the assessment, diagnosis, and treatment of problems of children and the developmentally disabled.

Psychology Practitioner Guidebooks

Editors

Arnold P. Goldstein, Syracuse University
Leonard Krasner, Stanford University & SUNY at Stony Brook
Sol L. Garfield, Washington University in St. Louis

Elsie M. Pinkston & Nathan L. Linsk—CARE OF THE ELDERLY: A Family Approach

Donald Meichenbaum—STRESS INOCULATION TRAINING

Sebastiano Santostefano—COGNITIVE CONTROL THERAPY WITH CHILDREN AND ADOLESCENTS

Lillie Weiss, Melanie Katzman & Sharlene Wolchik—TREATING BULIMIA: A Psychoeducational Approach

Edward B. Blanchard & Frank Andrasik—MANAGEMENT OF CHRONIC HEADACHES: A Psychological Approach

Raymond G. Romanczyk—CLINICAL UTILIZATION OF MICROCOMPUTER TECHNOLOGY

Philip H. Bornstein & Marcy T. Bornstein—MARITAL THERAPY: A Behavioral-Communications Approach

Michael T. Nietzel & Ronald C. Dillehay—PSYCHOLOGICAL CONSULTATION IN THE COURTROOM

Elizabeth B. Yost, Larry E. Beutler, M. Anne Corbishley & James R. Allender—GROUP COGNITIVE THERAPY: A Treatment Approach for Depressed Older Adults

Lillie Weiss—DREAM ANALYSIS IN PSYCHOTHERAPY

Edward A. Kirby & Liam K. Grimley—UNDERSTANDING AND TREATING ATTENTION DEFICIT DISORDER

Jon Eisenson—LANGUAGE AND SPEECH DISORDERS IN CHILDREN

Eva L. Feindler & Randolph B. Ecton—ADOLESCENT ANGER CONTROL: Cognitive-Behavioral Techniques

Michael C. Roberts—PEDIATRIC PSYCHOLOGY: Psychological Interventions and Strategies for Pediatric Problems

Daniel S. Kirschenbaum, William G. Johnson & Peter M. Stalonas, Jr.—TREATING CHILDHOOD AND ADOLESCENT OBESITY

W. Stewart Agras—EATING DISORDERS: Management of Obesity, Bulimia and Anorexia Nervosa

Ian H. Gotlib & Catherine A. Colby—TREATMENT OF DEPRESSION: An Interpersonal Systems Approach

Walter B. Pryzwansky & Robert N. Wendt—PSYCHOLOGY AS A PROFESSION: Foundations of Practice

Cynthia D. Belar, William W. Deardorff & Karen E. Kelly—THE PRACTICE OF CLINICAL HEALTH PSYCHOLOGY

Paul Karoly & Mark P. Jensen—MULTIMETHOD ASSESSMENT OF CHRONIC PAIN

William L. Golden, E. Thomas Dowd & Fred Friedberg—HYPNOTHERAPY: A Modern Approach

Patricia Lacks—BEHAVIORAL TREATMENT FOR PERSISTENT INSOMNIA

Arnold P. Goldstein & Harold Keller—AGGRESSIVE BEHAVIOR: Assessment and Intervention

C. Eugene Walker, Barbara L. Bonner & Keith L. Kaufman—THE PHYSICALLY AND SEXUALLY ABUSED CHILD: Evaluation and Treatment

Robert E. Becker, Richard G. Heimberg & Alan S. Bellack—SOCIAL SKILLS TRAINING TREATMENT FOR DEPRESSION

Richard F. Dangel & Richard A. Polster—TEACHING CHILD MANAGEMENT SKILLS

Albert Ellis, John F. McInerney, Raymond DiGiuseppe & Raymond Yeager—RATIONAL-EMOTIVE THERAPY WITH ALCOHOLICS AND SUBSTANCE ABUSERS

Johnny L. Matson & Thomas H. Ollendick—ENHANCING CHILDREN'S SOCIAL SKILLS: Assessment and Training

Edward B. Blanchard, John E. Martin & Patricia M. Dubbert—NON-DRUG TREATMENTS FOR ESSENTIAL HYPERTENSION

Samuel M. Turner & Deborah C. Beidel—TREATING OBSESSIVE-COMPULSIVE DISORDER

Alice W. Pope, Susan M. McHale & W. Edward Craighead—SELF-ESTEEM ENHANCEMENT WITH CHILDREN AND ADOLESCENTS

Jean E. Rhodes & Leonard A. Jason—PREVENTING SUBSTANCE ABUSE AMONG CHILDREN AND ADOLESCENTS

Gerald D. Oster, Janice E. Caro, Daniel R. Eagen & Margaret A. Lillo—ASSESSING ADOLESCENTS

Robin C. Winkler, Dirck W. Brown, Margaret van Keppel & Amy Blanchard—CLINICAL PRACTICE IN ADOPTION

Roger Poppen—BEHAVIORAL RELAXATION TRAINING AND ASSESSMENT

Michael D. LeBow—ADULT OBESITY THERAPY

Robert Paul Liberman, Kim T. Mueser, William J. DeRisi—SOCIAL SKILLS TRAINING FOR PSYCHIATRIC PATIENTS

Johnny L. Matson—TREATING DEPRESSION IN CHILDREN AND ADOLESCENTS